Dav

CENSORSHIP

or Freedom of Expression?

Nancy Day

LERNER PUBLICATIONS COMPANY • MINNEAPOLIS

Lerner Publications Company
A division of Lerner Publishing Group
241 First Avenue North
Minneapolis, MN 55401 U.S.A.

Website address: www.lernerbooks.com

Library of Congress Cataloging-in-Publication Data

Day, Nancy.
    Censorship / Nancy Day.
       p.   cm. — (Pro/Con)
    Includes bibliographical references and index.
    Summary: Examines the First Amendment, the issue of censorship in
publishing, schools, the arts and entertainment, and the Internet, and
government involvement.
    ISBN 0-8225-2628-X (alk. paper)
    1. Censorship—United States Juvenile literature.
[1. Censorship.] I. Title. II. Series: Pro/Con (Minneapolis, Minn.)
Z658.U5D39 2001
363.3'1—dc21   99-24215

Manufactured in the United States of America
1 2 3 4 5 6 – J/R – 06 05 04 03 02 01

CONTENTS

FOREWORD

If a nation expects to be ignorant and free, . . . it expects what never was and never will be.

Thomas Jefferson

Are you ready to participate in forming the policies of our government? Many issues are very confusing, and it can be difficult to know what to think about them or how to make a decision about them. Sometimes you must gather information about a subject before you can be informed enough to make a decision. Bernard Baruch, a prosperous American financier and an adviser to every president from Woodrow Wilson to Dwight D. Eisenhower, said, "If you can get all the facts, your judgment can be right; if you don't get all the facts, it can't be right."

But gathering information is only one part of the decision-making process. The way you interpret information is influenced by the values you have been taught since infancy—ideas about right and wrong, good and bad. Many of your values are shaped, or at least influenced, by how and where you grow up, by your race, sex, and religion, by how much money your family has. What your parents believe, what they read, and what you read and believe influence your decisions. The values of friends and teachers also affect what you think.

It's always good to listen to the opinions of people around you, but you will often confront contradictory points of view and points of view that are based not on fact, but on myth. John F. Kennedy, the 35th president of the United States, said, "The great enemy of the truth is very often not the lie—deliberate, contrived, and dishonest—but the myth—persistent, persuasive, and unrealistic." Eventually you will have to separate fact from myth and make up your own mind, make your own decisions. Because you are responsible for your decisions, it's

4

important to get as much information as you can. Then your decisions will be the right ones for you.

Making a fair and informed decision can be an exciting process, a chance to examine new ideas and different points of view. You live in a world that changes quickly and sometimes dramatically—a world that offers the opportunity to explore the ever-changing ground between yourself and others. Instead of forming a single, easy, or popular point of view, you might develop a rich and complex vision that offers new alternatives. Explore the many dimensions of an idea. Find kinship among an extensive range of opinions. Only after you've done this should you try to form your own opinions.

After you have formed an opinion about a particular subject, you may believe it is the only right decision. But some people will disagree with you and challenge your beliefs. They are not trying to antagonize you or put you down. They probably believe that they're right as sincerely as you believe you are. Thomas Macaulay, an English historian and author, wrote, "Men are never so likely to settle a question rightly as when they discuss it freely." In a democracy, the free exchange of ideas is not only encouraged, it's vital. Examining and discussing public issues and understanding opposing ideas are desirable and necessary elements of a free nation's ability to govern itself.

The Pro/Con series is designed to explore and examine different points of view on contemporary issues and to help you develop an understanding and appreciation of them. Most importantly, it will help you form your own opinions and make your own honest, informed decision.

Mary Winget
Series Editor

The woman above is protesting the U.S. government's decision to censor media coverage of the Gulf War in the early 1990s.

THE CENSORSHIP ISSUE

Steven Pico was a high school student in Island Trees, New York, when members of the school board demanded that certain books be removed from his school library. The board members had attended a conference at which a list of "objectionable books" had been distributed. Although both the superintendent of schools and the head librarian had objected, the board members removed nine books and restricted one. The board characterized the books as "anti-American, anti-Christian, anti-Sem[i]tic, and just plain filthy."

Pico was outraged. "For the first time in my life I felt that I understood what happened during the McCarthy era," he said. "After twelve years of schooling, my education had in many ways finally begun." When complaints led to media attention, the board issued a press release explaining, "[I]t is our duty, our moral obligation, to protect the children in our schools from this moral danger as surely as from physical and medical dangers." Pico and a group of other students sued the board, claiming that their First Amendment rights had been violated.[1] They had become victims of censorship.

THE FIRST AMENDMENT

When Congress voted to accept the Constitution in 1789, many people worried that the powerful, new, centralized government might trample the rights of the individual. In response to these concerns, James Madison created a series of amendments to the Constitution. In 1791, Congress approved the first ten amendments—which came to be known as the Bill of Rights. The amendments were meant to protect basic liberties and specific rights and freedoms.

Much debate took place during the drafting of the First Amendment. Several states already had provisions for freedom of speech and of the press, and they thought that the federal government shouldn't interfere with state laws. Congress, however, finally approved the First Amendment, which states: "Congress shall make no law respecting an establishment of religion, or prohibiting the free exercise thereof; or abridging the freedom of speech, or of the press; or the right of the people peaceably to assemble, and to petition the government for a redress of grievances." In this context, the word *speech* refers not only to the spoken or written word but to all forms of personal expression. The amendment imposes restrictions only on Congress, not the states. This has led some people to argue that states and local communities are free to set their own standards.

Even though freedom of speech and of the press are protected as fundamental rights, they can be restricted under certain conditions. For example, you cannot yell "Fire!" in a crowded theater if there is no fire. You cannot purposely print damaging lies about someone or even express them verbally in public. Words and images are considered legally obscene if "to the average person, applying contemporary community standards, the dominant theme of the material taken as a whole appeals to the prurient (unusual sexual) interest."

In some countries, criticizing the government or expressing certain beliefs is illegal. On December 10, 1948, the United Nations adopted a Universal Declaration of Human Rights to try to protect people's freedom of expression and other basic rights. Article 19

This painting shows Congress drafting the Bill of Rights in 1789. These first ten amendments to the Constitution protect citizens' basic rights, including freedom of speech, the press, assembly, and petition.

reads: "Everyone has the right to freedom of opinion and expression; this right includes freedom to hold opinions, without interference and to seek, receive, and impart information and ideas through any media regardless of frontiers."[2]

WHAT IS CENSORSHIP?

Censorship occurs when the government, special interest groups, or private individuals impose their moral or political values on others by suppressing words, images, or ideas that they find objectionable. Censorship is the restriction of what people may say, hear, write, read, or see. It can affect books, newspapers, magazines, movies, radio and television programs, speeches, music, painting, sculpture, photography, and other arts.

The Puritans' intolerance for so-called "witches" is a prime example of censorship of deed and thought in colonial America. People perceived as witches were brought to trial and often hanged or burned.

Censorship can take place in various ways. It can occur before the work is made available to the public, such as when a publisher refuses to produce a book, a movie company rejects a script, or a museum declines an exhibit because some people think the content is controversial or objectionable. Or censorship can take place after a work becomes public—when a book is removed from a library or bookstore because some people find its content objectionable.

Sometimes, the censor removes or destroys a work. In other cases, a work may be banned, or made illegal to produce or sell. Another method of censorship involves treating the work in question differently, either by putting it in a special area or requiring parental permission in order for a child to obtain it.

Even people who believe strongly in freedom of expression are sometimes offended by certain kinds of speech. And the kinds of speech people find offensive can vary. For example, a person who thinks it is silly to cover a nude statue might want to remove a book containing the word *nigger* from the school library. Someone else could be comfortable with such language but might want to remove a book about witchcraft because the topic offends his or her religious beliefs.

Freedom of speech is always easier to grant to those who hold opinions similar to your own than to those who have opposing opinions. The Puritans who fled the religious intolerance of England for the freedom of America showed their own intolerance when they burned "witches" in Salem. American patriots had no qualms about silencing Tory sympathizers—colonists who remained faithful to King George III of England—

with tar and feathers. Religious Right groups often favor censorship of sexually oriented materials but want freedom to distribute their texts on street corners and in public schools. Universities may protect free political expression yet severely restrict "politically incorrect" speech.

WHAT GETS CENSORED

In ancient Rome, censors were magistrates who counted the number of people who were Roman citizens. The Roman government used the count, called the census, to collect taxes, raise armies, and regulate voting. Eventually the duties of the censor also included setting moral standards for Roman citizens. Censors had authority over what people did, what they said, and what they wrote.

For the most part, censors still believe they are protecting the morals of society. Most materials that are challenged contain images, words, or ideas that some organization or individual finds immoral and wants to restrict. Books, movies, and television programs are frequent targets, but other media can also be censored.

Advertising is sometimes censored. The government prohibits advertisements for certain kinds of products and restricts what can be said about others. Advertisements for cigarettes and liquor, for example, are banned from television. Newspaper and magazine publishers and television networks maintain standards that outline what they consider acceptable advertising. They routinely refuse ads that might be considered offensive or controversial to their audiences. For many years, they wouldn't accept advertisements for feminine hygiene products, and most still reject ads for condoms.

Public opinion plays a large role in what is considered acceptable in advertising. When the American Foundation for AIDS Research wanted to create a public service advertisement that would attract attention, they chose the slogan "Prayer Won't Cure AIDS. Research Will." Ads were pasted on buses in 19 cities. Some transit agencies, responding to complaints, took the ads down and the foundation ended up canceling the entire campaign. Jesse Oliver, a board member of one of the transit agencies that pulled the ad, later said, "I'm concerned whether we bowed to pressure and exercised censorship because a small group didn't agree with the message."[3]

Sometimes you can tell when something has been

Shops that sell pornographic materials may meet with resistance from protesters.

censored, but many times you can't. For instance, if a news director decides to cut a story about a local clinic that provides abortions, viewers will never know. Similarly, if a teacher changes a book assignment after hearing that the work in question is controversial, students will probably never even know that the title had been considered.

One of the basic questions raised in any discussion of censorship is whether anyone has or should have the authority to decide what material is to be restricted. As a vice principal in Hawkins County, Tennessee, put it: "It boils down to who is going to tell who to read what." [4]

HATE AND VIOLENCE

Do you want to know how to booby trap a door handle or make an alarm-clock time bomb? Do you want to learn how to make illegal drugs? Books that contain information on sabotage, surveillance, weaponry, drug making, and explosives are available through the mail, on the Internet, and at some libraries. Should the public have access to information about dangerous—or even illegal—devices? Should we maintain the right to free speech and free press no matter what the content is and what the consequences might be?

Activist Tom Blair says that views like his are routinely suppressed. He defends those who question the reality of the Holocaust and those who oppose third-world immigration. Many people would label Tom Blair a racist or a Nazi. "Censorship is not little old ladies complaining about dirty pictures on the Internet," he says. "Censorship is very powerful people stopping political, historical, and religious speech they don't like."[5] White supremacist groups distributing "nigger jokes," antigay groups with "fagbashing" Web pages, and other organizations that fan the flames of hatred are protected by the First Amendment. But should all these voices be allowed to be heard?

Hate speech uses hurtful images or words (usually based on a person's race, religion, or sexual orientation) to threaten, intimidate, or attack. The words may be directed at one person or at a whole class of people. Hate speech may lead to violence, either because the person making the threat acts on it or because the target of the threat retaliates. Words that instigate violence are called "fighting words." This concept is based on the 1942 Supreme Court decision, *Chaplinsky v. New Hampshire,* which held that speech that encourages violence is not protected. Hate speech that does not incite violence, however, is protected by law.

Some cities and institutions created "speech codes" to control hate speech. For example, St. Paul, Minnesota's hate-crime law called for:

> [special punishment of any person who] places on public or private property a symbol, object, appellation [name], characterization, or graffiti, including, but not limited to, a burning cross or Nazi swastika, which one knows or has reasonable grounds to know arouses anger, alarm, or resentment in others on the basis of race, color, creed, religion, or gender.

Then in June 1992, the Supreme Court ruling in *R.A.V. v. City of St. Paul, Minnesota* struck down the city's ordinance against hate speech. Robert A. Viktora, whose initials appear in the case name, had been

Neo-Nazi groups (above) protest at a Gay Pride Parade in New York City. Members of the Ku Klux Klan (right), a white supremacist organization, recruit their children into the ranks.

convicted under the St. Paul law after he burned a cross on the lawn of a black family living in a mostly white neighborhood. Although the justices agreed that the cross burning was "reprehensible," they thought that "St. Paul has sufficient means at its disposal to prevent such behavior without adding the First Amendment to the fire." [6]

Politically incorrect speech, sometimes called "slighting words," doesn't generally lead to violence but is sometimes dealt with dramatically—particularly if the speaker is a public figure. In 1999, after playing a song by a black singer, a popular radio personality commented, "No wonder people drag them behind trucks," a reference to James Byrd Jr., a black man who had been dragged to his death in a racially motivated murder. The radio personality was fired for making the remark. This type of speech promotes stereotypes and demeans people through insensitivity rather than hate.[7]

SELF-CENSORSHIP

Some censorship is *self*-imposed in anticipation of public backlash. It is the result of thousands of small decisions, minor changes, and altered courses taken by individuals or institutions, based on their own fears and perceptions. This form of censorship is difficult to pin down and sometimes even hard to detect.

College textbooks on children's literature often contain chapters on censorship. In *Children's Literature in the Elementary School,* educator Charlotte S. Huck wrote, "A more subtle and frightening kind of censorship is that kind practiced voluntarily by librarians and teachers. If a book has come under negative scrutiny in a nearby town, it is carefully placed under the librarian's desk until the controversy dies down."[8]

Misha Arenstein, a teacher with over 20 years of experience, admits, "I indulge in self-censorship—a practice widely prevalent in many schools. Coming across a mild expletive, an off-color word, or a situation involving realistic sexual interest, I often set a book aside. Will my administrators welcome the chance to defend my academic freedom, I silently ponder?"[9]

Nazis burned over 20,000 literary works believed to contain "non-Aryan" ideas at "The Great Ceremony" on May 10, 1933, in Berlin, Germany.

CENSORSHIP THROUGHOUT HISTORY

On May 10, 1933, five thousand singing students ended a torchlight parade with a huge book burning in Nazi Germany. A crowd of 25,000 watched the works of Albert Einstein, Sigmund Freud, Marcel Proust, Ernest Hemingway, Helen Keller, and Jack London go up in flames. Joseph Goebbels, Hitler's propaganda minister, spoke into a microphone on a podium overlooking the fire. "Jewish intellectualism is dead," he declared. "The German folk soul can again express itself. These flames not only illuminate the final end of the old era; they also light up the new."[1]

Mary Heaton Vorse, an American journalist, saw the situation differently. She wrote, "Bright as fire they mount upwards, farther and farther they soar, high above the blaze. One page goes on and on; it mounts bright and defiant as if it said, 'You can't burn me. You can't burn thought.'"[2] Nevertheless, the desire to suppress thought, particularly when expressed in public media such as books, has been a part of life throughout history.

THE EARLY YEARS

Censorship has probably been in existence since humans began to communicate with each other. In early cultures, religious and political authorities often placed restrictions on the general population. Rigid guidelines for acceptable art appeared in Egypt as early as 3400 B.C. and existed virtually unchanged for more than three thousand years. The poet Ovid was exiled from ancient Rome because his *Ars Amatoria* had offended the moral sensibilities of Emperor Augustus. The ancient Greek city-state of Sparta banned poetry and other reading material that didn't deal with "useful" topics, like agriculture and commerce.

Some of history's great thinkers, such as the ancient Greek philosophers Plato and Aristotle, supported censorship. Plato (ca 428–347 B.C.) thought that because art has the power to intensify emotions, not just release them, a "drastic censor" should control it. Aristotle (384–322 B.C.) said that young people should be protected not only from words but also from pictures. "We must forbid looking at unseemly pictures," he wrote.[3] In 213 B.C., Chinese emperor Shi Huang Di burned *The Analects* of the philosopher Confucius and nearly all the other books in China in an attempt to destroy old loyalties and ideas.

During the Middle Ages in western Europe, almost all artistic expression was commissioned by the government or the Catholic Church. Artists designed their work to please their patrons. Before the invention of the printing press in the 15th century, literature was also produced primarily through patronage.

In 1538, the English monarchy established licensing

laws to allow the government to control what was printed. In 1559, Queen Elizabeth I ordered that no book could be published without approval. At one point, royal agents routinely searched London printing houses to see whether they were printing anything illegal. Forbidden books were burned by the hangman, as though ideas could be executed like people.[4]

In 1643, the English government issued a censorship edict that required all books be submitted to an official censor before publication. John Milton, a well-known poet, responded by publishing (without approval) *Areopagitica,* a pamphlet that criticized censorship. He

Greek philosopher Plato (left) *was in favor of a "drastic censor" of the arts.* **Emperor Shi Huang Di had nearly all the books in China burned, including The Analects** *by philosopher* **Confucius (above).**

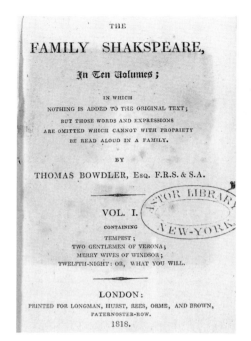

THE

FAMILY SHAKSPEARE,

In Ten Volumes;

IN WHICH
NOTHING IS ADDED TO THE ORIGINAL TEXT;
BUT THOSE WORDS AND EXPRESSIONS
ARE OMITTED WHICH CANNOT WITH PROPRIETY
BE READ ALOUD IN A FAMILY.

BY

THOMAS BOWDLER, Esq. F.R.S. & S.A.

VOL. I.

CONTAINING

TEMPEST;
TWO GENTLEMEN OF VERONA;
MERRY WIVES OF WINDSOR;
TWELFTH-NIGHT: OR, WHAT YOU WILL.

LONDON:
PRINTED FOR LONGMAN, HURST, REES, ORME, AND BROWN,
PATERNOSTER-ROW.
1818.

Bowdler's Family Shakespeare was a popular version of the bard's work. Thomas Bowdler edited Shakespeare's work in 1818 for what he considered to be offensive content.

argued that he who kills a man "kills a reasonable crea-ture," but he who destroys a good book "kills reason it-self."[5]

As political and religious censorship eased, concern over morality increased. Censorship began to move from the government to the publishers, editors, writers, and, in some cases, even the readers. People were en-couraged to censor their own reading through books such as *Bowdler's Family Shakespeare,* published in London in 1818 and widely circulated throughout the United States. Thomas Bowdler published works by Shakespeare and other authors, but he edited out refer-ences to sex and any other passages that he believed "unfit to be read aloud by a gentleman to a company of ladies."[6] From this practice comes the term *bowdler-ized*, meaning edited to remove vulgar material, resulting in a distortion of the original work.

A MAN WITH A MISSION: ANTHONY COMSTOCK

Anthony Comstock arrived in New York City in 1867 with five dollars in his pocket. In 1872, he noticed that fellow employees at a dry-goods store were passing around "dirty" books and pictures. He decided to do something about it.

In 1873, Comstock founded the New York Society for the Suppression of Vice. He said that the printed page was Satan's chief weapon to ruin the family and that "a single book or a single picture may taint forever the soul of the person who reads or sees it."[7]

Comstock lobbied Congress for a law that would allow the U.S. Postal Service to prohibit indecent material from being sent through the mail. In 1873 Congress passed the Comstock Law, and Anthony Comstock became a special agent of the Postal Service to implement the new law. At age 28, he had become the most powerful censor in the United States. His motto was "Morals, Not Art or Literature."[8]

Comstock later bragged that he had seized 134,000 pounds of books during his first six months on the job. He did not discriminate between literary classics and dime novels. "Garbage smells none the less rank and offensive because deposited in a marble fount or a gold or silver urn," he said.[9] In 1905, Comstock had George Bernard Shaw's classic *Man and Superman* removed to the reserve shelf at the New York Public Library. Shaw exploded with the now-famous exclamation

"Comstockery!" and declared that Comstock's enforced prudery was "the world's standing joke at the expense of the United States."[10] Nevertheless, Comstock continued his campaign until his death in 1915.

THE VICE SOCIETIES

The vice-society movement that Comstock began was partly a response to fears about contemporary city life after the Civil War (1861–1865). As has happened during other periods of social and economic unrest, people reacted by pushing for a return to the security and stability of a strict moral structure.

The general public welcomed vice societies as a responsible cause that would cleanse communities and protect children. "We are fighting . . . to protect the young," the Watch and Ward Society stated in 1898.[11]

The idea that offensive publications were harmful to children was supported by doctors of the time. In 1879, Elizabeth Blackwell, America's first female medical doctor, wrote that "the dangers arising from vicious literature of any kind cannot be overestimated by parents. . . . The permanent and incalculable injury which is done to the young mind by vicious reading is proved by all that we know about the structure and methods of growth of the human mind."[12]

Censorship was widely accepted, and few people questioned the practice. An editorial in a British library journal in 1922 that was praised by the *American Library Journal* stated, "We librarians do not like to pose as moralists, but we have no objection to taking upon ourselves the duties of the physician. And as doctors, we can have no hesitation in sterilizing our shelves, in cutting out and casting from us the morbid, neurotic, wrongheaded, decadent books, of which there are too many written nowadays."[13]

BACKLASH

Eventually, anticensorship feelings began to build. In 1923, author Thomas Dixon spoke at an American Booksellers Association meeting in New York City. He described censorship as "the most odious word in the English language." He said, "It comes down to us from Europe, wet with tears, reeking with the groans and anguish of martyrs through the centuries . . . I . . . believe

In 1935, John Sumner (middle, with hat), president of the Society for the Suppression of Vice, watched over this book burning in the cellar of New York City's police headquarters.

with every fiber of my soul and body, that God Almighty never made a man or woman big enough, broad enough, wise enough, strong enough, to be entrusted with the tremendous power that is put in the hands of a censor."[14]

Librarians started to reexamine their role. Librarian Margery Bedinger asked her colleagues in 1931, "Who, after all, are we to set ourselves up as capable of saying what will or will not harm another person? We have thought that upon us lay the heavy burden of guarding the morals of youth, 90 percent of whom could tell us many things!"[15]

By the 1930s, literary censorship was decreasing. Vice societies began to disband, and the public called for changes in the obscenity laws. Individual moralists and local officials no longer had the power to suppress literature. Attention shifted to a new issue—the power of the federal government to control the free circulation of books.

The shift began with an examination of the United States Customs Bureau. The bureau had had the authority to prevent "obscene" materials from entering the United States since the Tariff of 1842. In 1929, a routine renewal of the censorship provisions of the tariff bill met with objections when the House of Representatives wanted to alter it. The House voted to extend the provisions of the bill to include materials "advocating or urging treason, insurrection, or forcible resistance to any law of the United States, or containing any threat to take the life or inflict bodily harm upon the President of the United States."[16]

Individuals and organizations such as the American

Civil Liberties Union (ACLU) immediately protested the attempt to impose political censorship. But Senator Bronson M. Cutting of New Mexico thought the entire section of the tariff bill was "unsound." When the final version of the law (which became known as the Smoot-Hawley Tariff) was passed, Section 305 had been amended. The tariff no longer contained the section on treason. It did, however, establish a more liberal policy on obscene materials, with the courts—not Customs employees—as the final authority on what was permissible. By 1935, any book printed by an established publisher was freely admitted into the United States.

In the 1950s and 1960s, a new group of publishers began to publish materials well beyond the limits formerly accepted, and society was again in a period of unrest. Senator Joseph McCarthy's "witch hunts" for supposed Communists during the 1950s spurred the call for increased morality and tighter social controls. By the 1964 presidential campaign, the Republican Party's platform pledged "enactment of legislation, despite Democratic opposition, to curb the flow through our mails of obscene material which has flourished into a multimillion-dollar obscenity racket."[17]

Since that time, the censorship issue has become even more complex. New forms of expression, such as performance art, rap music, experimental film, and the Internet, have created new methods of communication and revolutionary technologies for challenging society's boundaries on what it is willing to tolerate. Conflict still continues between those who wish to exercise freedom of speech and of the press and those who want to curb such freedoms.

These literary classics have been banned in schools for perceived violent, sexual, or verbally offensive content.

CENSORSHIP GOES TO SCHOOL

In 1993, 15-year-old Joseph Smith opened *The Great Santini,* one of the books he had been assigned for his English class. He was shocked by author Pat Conroy's vivid description of a rape. The book also included a vulgar parody of the "Hail Mary" and other passages Smith considered offensive. He objected to the assignment and was given an alternative book to read. But Smith thought *The Great Santini* was not appropriate for *any* high school student.

He filed a formal objection with the school district and participated in a hearing to discuss the issue. "I believe," said Smith, "in the rights of students not to have to grow up before their time, not to have perversions shoved down their throats, not to have violence smashed in their faces in the name of education."

Opponents argued that Smith was trying to control what others could or could not read—acting as an uninvited censor. Smith asked why the district couldn't find books that present positive role models and avoid books that show the unsavory aspects of the world.[1]

Robert Duvall starred in the film version of The Great Santini, *the book that high school student Joseph Smith hoped to have banned.*

The issue of selection rather than censorship is at the core of many of the arguments about school and library books. Many people argue that since most school and library budgets are limited, why spend scarce funds on books that may be controversial? Karen Jo Gounaud, founder of Family Friendly Libraries, argues that good judgment in book selection is not censorship.

But what constitutes good judgment? And who is qualified to make that judgment for other readers? Some of the world's greatest literature has also been among the most controversial.

SCHOOLS AS BATTLEGROUNDS

Censorship targets change as society's values and prejudices change. In 1959, Garth Williams's children's book *The Rabbits' Wedding* was attacked by white parents in Florida and Alabama because it showed a black rabbit and a white rabbit getting married.[2] The parents thought the book promoted the idea of mixing the races, which they opposed at that time. In more recent years, books that contain racist content have been found objectionable. Even books that are not racist may be removed if people object to them. For example, in 1998, a book called *Nappy Hair* became a target when a white teacher chose it for a racially mixed third-grade class. The book, written by a black woman, uses humor to tell the story of an African American girl and her hair. Black parents objected to the book, and both the book and the teacher were removed.[3]

The black and white rabbits in The Rabbits' Wedding dressed up with dandelions at their "interracial" wedding.

Many school censorship cases involve the Religious Right—often fundamentalist Christians—objecting to materials that challenge or conflict with their beliefs. They object to books that contain explicit information about sex and sexual orientation, present evolution as fact, promote all cultures and peoples of the world as equal, encourage non-Christian rituals or practices (such as meditation), discuss witchcraft, or promote a view of the world that is not based on the Bible.

Fear of censorship has affected the content of school textbooks. Some school districts—and occasionally entire states—sometimes refuse to buy textbooks that contain information that might be considered controversial. Some health books sidestep information on birth control and sexually transmitted diseases (STDs)

The Chocolate War *by Robert Cromier has been banned by several schools for its realistic descriptions of young teenagers' desires and bodily functions.*

for fear of objections from religious groups. Many biology texts don't cover evolution adequately, and some don't mention it at all, because it challenges the religious notion of divine creation. In August 1999, the Kansas Board of Education voted 6-4 to adopt new standards for science teaching that eliminate evolution as an underlying principle of biology in public schools. That same year, the state of Kentucky deleted the word *evolution* from school curriculum guidelines. Kentucky State Department of Education officials substituted the words *change over time.*[4]

Schools sometimes have difficulty protecting the sensibilities of some students and parents without restricting the freedoms of others. Arthur J. Kropp, president of People for the American Way, a constitutional liberties organization, said, "In the typical censorship incident, an individual or very small group—sometimes parents, sometimes not—attempts to dictate to an entire community what all children can or cannot read or learn. To most observers, that kind of 'dictating' crosses the line into censorship."[5]

PROTECTING IMPRESSIONABLE MINDS

People who favor restricting children's reading material believe that teachers and librarians have a responsibility to "protect" students from language and ideas they consider objectionable. These people believe certain books are hurtful or dangerous, and they want to protect students from them in the same way they would protect children from physical harm.

One long-time censorship target has been Mark Twain's novel *Adventures of Huckleberry Finn.* The story is set in pre-Civil War Missouri and, being true to the time and setting, one of the characters, an African-American man, is frequently referred to as "Miss Watson's big nigger, named Jim." One of the most important points made by the book is that while the white adults of the town see Jim only as a "nigger," Huck gets to know Jim as a person, and the relationship changes his life. Although the book has become a classic, many people are uncomfortable exposing children to the word *nigger,* which is considered a racist term.

To what extent should children's books present a realistic view of the world? Robert Cromier's *The Chocolate War,* published in 1974, immediately became controversial. The young characters sweated, urinated, daydreamed about girls' breasts, used bad language, and experienced sexual feelings. In short, they were like real kids—perhaps too real for some adults.

The Chocolate War has been challenged in many schools. Parent Nancy Mowrey told the school board review committee in New Milford, Connecticut, that the book contained "crude and blasphemous" language and unnecessary "sexual activities." She asked, "Why do we find it necessary to fill our children's heads full of this?"[6] Parents in other districts objected to the book's negativity, critical view of the Catholic Church, and lack of positive role models.

Author Zibby Oneal, in an essay called "They Tell You to Do Your Own Thing, but They Don't Mean It," said, "No one is required to like *The Chocolate War* or to agree with its conclusion or to want to take its characters home to dinner, but nobody has the right to deny

Judy Blume's popular books expose children and young adults to frustrating aspects of growing up, including self-image problems and sexual situations.

it to someone else. The decision to pull a book from the shelf is dangerous business, and most dangerous of all when that decision involves the young. We try to teach young people about First Amendment rights then deny them a book."[7]

Judy Blume is a writer whose books are frequent targets of censorship. "I think that adults are so uncomfortable about their own sexuality that they can't begin to deal with their children's," says Blume. "Adults have always been suspicious of books that kids like," she says. "It seems as if some adults choose to forget what mattered to them when they were children. If they remembered, they might not have this warped view of what's 'good' for kids." She also suggests that "Some parents are frightened by the idea of exposing their children to new ideas, ideas that are different from their own."[8]

Some of Blume's critics argue that books can destroy a child's innocence and expose the young reader to aspects of the world better left alone. It can be damaging, they say, to present children with negative, sexual, or violent material before they are ready to handle it.

Author Jean Karl disagrees. She says, "If we can no longer picture teenage sexual explorations, the trauma of abortion, their terrors of drug addiction after its initial pleasures, the things that are really wrong with our society, and lives that are not lived in a perfect suburb, then we are lying to our children and forcing them into cultural blindness that could eventually shatter the fabric of the nation."[9]

WHO CHOOSES TEXTBOOKS?

In 1961, Texas residents Mel and Norma Gabler objected to the fact that their children's textbooks appeared to endorse a one-world government while downplaying the role of the United States and the importance of Christianity. Although neither had special training in education, they decided to get involved in the process and rapidly became a major influence in the selection of school textbooks.

In 23 states, including Texas, a textbook committee determines which books will be used throughout the entire state. Publishers try especially hard to get their books accepted in Texas, one of the largest markets for textbooks in the country.

When the Gablers found textbooks they didn't like, they persuaded members of the Texas selection committee to reject the books or demand revisions. In some cases, publishers even produced special editions of

Offensive language is the most frequent reason for challenging, restricting, removing or banning books. Some titles deemed offensive because of "obscene," "racist," or "sexist" language include:

The Adventures of Huckleberry Finn

The Canterbury Tales

Death of a Salesman

The Giving Tree

Mother Goose

Of Mice and Men

Snow Falling on Cedars

Their Eyes Were Watching God

CELEBRATE

THE FREEDOM

TO READ

This poster from the Foundation for Free Expression promotes the reading of banned books. The works, including several classics, have been banned due to offensive or sexual situations and/or violent language.

books for the state of Texas. "The publishers are friends," says Norma Gabler. "They go out of their way to be nice to us."[10]

Eventually the Gablers began to mail textbook reviews to parents and teachers across the country. The couple objects to anything that promotes the belief that humans, not God, determine values and guide the

To ensure the inclusion of Christian values in textbooks, Norma and Mel Gabler, shown here in the 1980s, succeeded in having textbooks censored, edited, and sometimes republished for the Texas Textbook Committee.

world. Parents often use the Gablers's reviews to identify books that might be challenged in their own individual districts.

Greg R. Jesson, formerly the public policy research manager of Focus on the Family, an organization that promotes Bible-based education, says that parents who express concern over school textbooks should not be labeled censors. He thinks that if parents cannot speak out about what their children are being taught, then their First Amendment rights are being denied. Authors can write anything they please, says Jesson, but parents have the right to protect their children from "harmful literature."[11]

STUDENT NEWSPAPERS

Years ago, most school newspapers were closely reviewed and restricted by administrators. Discussions about drug use, drinking, racial tensions, and criticism of school management or faculty were rarely allowed. In the 1960s, however, battles began to develop between student journalists and administrators. Students had become politically involved and wanted to write about issues they considered more important than when the next pep rally was scheduled.

In 1969, the Supreme Court's decision in *Tinker v. Des Moines Independent School District* affirmed the right of students to express themselves. The case involved a student's right to wear a black armband to protest the Vietnam War. Justice Abe Fortas declared, "It can hardly be argued that either students or teachers shed their constitutional rights to freedom of speech or expression at the schoolhouse gate."[12] This ruling—and later cases in lower courts—extended the right of free expression to student newspapers. To censor a school newspaper, the administration had to be able to prove that the expression would cause a material and substantial disruption of school activities or an invasion of the rights of others.

Then in 1988, the Supreme Court's decision in

Hazelwood School District v. Kuhlmeier gave school administrators greater leeway to censor student expression. The case involved an administration's right to control the content of a high school newspaper. The decision determined that a student newspaper is not a public forum, and therefore school authorities can restrict its content. Administrators have to show only that they have reasonable educational reasons for censoring a student publication.

Since *Hazelwood,* there has been a dramatic rise in censorship incidents in schools across the country. Acts of censorship can take many forms. Mark Goodman, executive director of the Student Press Law Center, says, "It may be outright censorship—they can't publish a story—or an attempt to punish, either the students or in some cases the teacher or the adviser or taking away money from the publication or trying to discontinue it for the future or any one of a thousand different avenues."[13] To avoid legal problems and negative publicity, some administrators have used the excuse of budget cuts to decrease publications or eliminate them entirely.

The *Hazelwood* decision has had a chilling effect. Students have become more cautious about what they publish. Rather than risk that an article be rejected by an adviser or principal, students sometimes choose to censor themselves.

On election day in 1997, a novel form of censorship emerged at the Berkeley campus of the University of California. Almost the entire press run, 24,000 copies, of the *Daily Californian* was stolen because the paper contained an editorial in support of the proposition to end affirmative action. In 1993, 60 black students stole nearly all 14,000 copies of a University of Pennsylvania paper that they said promoted "institutional racism." Nearly 100 college papers reported major thefts within a four-year period.[14]

What do the administrations do to fight censorship by theft? In the Pennsylvania case, none of the students involved were punished, and the guard who chased them was reprimanded.

What Everyone Should Know About The Movie Rating System.

GENERAL AUDIENCES
G
G | GENERAL AUDIENCES
All Ages Admitted

Nothing that would offend parents for viewing by children.

PARENTAL GUIDANCE SUGGESTED
PG
PG | PARENTAL GUIDANCE SUGGESTED
SOME MATERIAL MAY NOT BE SUITABLE FOR CHILDREN

Parents urged to give "parental guidance." May contain some material parents might not like for their young children.

PARENTS STRONGLY CAUTIONED
PG-13
PG-13 | PARENTS STRONGLY CAUTIONED
Some Material May Be Inappropriate for Children Under 13

Parents are urged to be cautious. Some material may be inappropriate for pre-teenagers.

RESTRICTED
R
R | RESTRICTED
UNDER 17 REQUIRES ACCOMPANYING PARENT OR ADULT GUARDIAN

Contains some adult material. Parents are urged to learn more about the film before taking their young children with them.

NO ONE 17 AND UNDER ADMITTED
NC-17
NC-17 | NO ONE 17 AND UNDER ADMITTED

Patently adult. Children are not admitted.

Movie ratings became the norm in 1968. The original M (mature audiences) has changed to PG and PG-13, while X (under 17 not admitted) has become NC-17.

AN EYE ON THE ENTERTAINMENT MEDIA

One evening in 1997, eight-year-old Tynisha Gathers and three other children in Bridgeport, Connecticut, watched a videotape about four women who robbed banks. After the video, Tynisha asked one of the girls to shoot her like the person in the movie had been shot. The girl took a .380-caliber semiautomatic handgun and shot Tynisha in the forehead, killing her.

What went wrong here? Was the problem a powerful weapon in the hands of a child or fictional violence producing real-life tragedy? If the children hadn't seen the movie, would Tynisha still be alive?[1]

THE TIMES THEY ARE A CHANGIN'
In 1975, under pressure from Congress and the Federal Communications Commission, television networks designated 8:00 to 9:00 P.M. as the "Family Hour," a period during which only programming suitable for all ages would be broadcast. The Writers Guild of America and other groups challenged the rule, saying it violated

the First Amendment, and won. But that time slot became generally accepted as the Family Hour anyway. It became an unwritten rule that only "wholesome" programs would be shown during that period.

In recent years, the concept of the Family Hour has almost disappeared. Prime time shows are packed with cursing children, adulterous adults, and sexually active teenagers. A four-week survey of Family Hour programs in 1995 found 40 instances of premarital sex, eight treatments of extramarital sex, seven references to sexual issues, and many examples of vulgar language.[2]

A study of 1,351 randomly selected television programs in 1997 and 1998 found that 56 percent of the shows reviewed had either sexual talk or actions. Soap operas and talk shows—which are daytime shows— averaged over 80 percent.[3]

Concern over the content of television shows led to the development of a rating system similar to that used by the motion picture industry. But researchers studying the effects of violent and sexually explicit television programs on children found that rating systems actually tend to attract young viewers to the more mature programs. One of the researchers, Joanne Cantor, called it the "forbidden fruit syndrome."[4] In addition, a study conducted in 1998 found that while the age-based portion of the ratings (TV-6, TV-14, and so forth) was being applied accurately, the content designation (V for violence, for example) was not being widely used.[5]

What role does personal responsibility play? Some people think that parents should determine what programs are suitable for their children. Other people think that objectionable material doesn't belong on television at all. Many children are unsupervised during part of the day because their parents work. Who will guide their television viewing? One possible solution is the V-chip, a computer chip installed in each television set or cable box that allows parents to block programs they find objectionable for their children without interfering with the choices of other people. There are also electronic devices, such as the "TV Guardian," that automatically replace offensive language with more acceptable terms.

IT'S HOLLYWOOD!
Almost since the first moving pictures became available, people have realized what an impact films can

Tim Collings invented the V-chip, a computer chip that parents may use to block out specific television programs.

The one-minute film The Kiss, *released in 1896, included three kisses that many critics found too passionate.*

have. *The Kiss*, released in 1896, was only one minute long, but it caused quite a sensation. One magazine said, "The spectacle of the prolonged pasturing on each other's lips" was "beastly" enough on stage but "magnified to gargantuan proportions and repeated three times over it is absolutely disgusting."[6]

When feature-length films began to appear, those depicting prostitution, birth control, abortion, venereal disease, and true crime all came under attack by moralists, particularly when children were allowed to see them. People argued that young people "were given ideas" by seeing crimes and sex in the movies. "Movies are schools of vice and crime . . . offering trips to hell for [a] nickel," said Reverend Wilbur Crafts.[7] However, the industry argued that the criminals and villains were always punished in the end, so the films should actually act as deterrents.

On November 4, 1907, Chicago became the first major city to establish a system of prior censorship by authorizing police to deny a permit to any film they judged "immoral" or "obscene." The moviemakers went to court to block the censorship move, but the Illinois Supreme Court ruled that the city had a right to ensure decency, particularly because the low cost of admission encouraged children to attend.[8]

Growing protest by clergy in New York City led to Mayor George B. McClellan closing all movie houses on December 24, 1908. The industry was able to obtain an injunction allowing them to reopen, but the attention resulted in the establishment of the National Board of Censorship of Motion Pictures in March 1909. The board had no legal power, but the industry cooperated with it to avoid any future government censorship. The liberality of the board irritated critics who continued to call for broad government censorship.

In 1915, the Supreme Court decision in *Mutual Film Corporation v. Industrial Commission of Ohio* denied the industry's position that films were protected by the First Amendment. The Court ruled that film is a theatrical performance rather than a published work. Following that decision, it seemed there would be a flood of censorship boards—each with its own standards and preferences.

In 1922, the Motion Picture Producers and Distributors of America (MPPDA) was established, and William Harrison Hays was appointed its spokesperson and lobbyist. At the time, approximately one hundred individual censorship bills were being introduced in 37 states. "When you eat your fish or your meat, or see your child drink her glass of milk, isn't it good to know they have been censored, so they will nourish and not poison?" asked B. Preston Clark, a Boston leader of one censorship coalition.[9] Hays created a voluntary system of censorship (including what became known as the "Don'ts and Be Carefuls") within the film industry, but protests continued. The advent of talking pictures created even more problems.

During World War I, American Catholic bishops created the National War Council, with the goal of protecting the faith and morals of military personnel. Through the War Council, the church became involved with the army's efforts to use "social hygiene" films to discourage the spread of venereal disease. When these films were released commercially, the church opposed the move.

The church's influence grew. By 1923, the motion picture committee of the National Catholic Welfare Conference (which was the new name for the National War Council after World War I) was issuing monthly lists of approved films. The International Federation of Catholic Alumnae, a group made up of graduates from Catholic high schools and colleges, also issued lists of recommended films. These "white lists" reviewed only recommended films and ignored all others.

In 1929, a small group of Catholics suggested that

films be censored during production, thus eliminating the need for censorship boards later. There would be a Catholic Code to ensure that films were made "properly." The code went beyond forbidding nudity and sexual content. It required films to promote the idea that the church, the government, and the family were the basis of a good society.

A small group of film producers made a counterproposal. Films, they said, were simply a reflection of contemporary life. Audiences went to see films they liked and didn't patronize the ones they didn't like. Therefore, there was no need for an outside board to determine what audiences wanted. Instead, the producers offered to use "good taste" and to make an effort to include "compensating moral values" in all their films.[10] This proposal got little support.

Studios learned that they could often avoid trouble and maybe even get on the white lists by making a few alterations in their films. One studio changed the villain in The *Hunchback of Notre Dame* so he was no longer a priest. Another removed a crucifix from a wall in *The Merry Widow* and eliminated the line "His father was so lazy he married a widow with six children" from *Foiled.* Some of the changes were small, but others were not.[11]

By 1933, the tide had turned in favor of actively blacklisting unapproved movies. The powerful Cardinal George W. Mundelein, of the Chicago diocese, appointed Father Daniel Lord to draft the Catholic Code. Lord said that encouraging the film industry to reform through white lists was a waste of time since one could record all the recommended films "on the back of a postage stamp and have room left over for the Declaration of Independence."[12]

In 1934, the Catholic Church established the Legion of Decency to blacklist any films it found offensive. The legion began to pick up additional support from non-Catholics. Upon hearing that an estimated 5 million people were boycotting films, the movie industry began to panic. Industry representatives struck a deal with the church. A new Production Code Administration (PCA) was established. No film could begin production until the PCA had approved the script. Any film that didn't have the PCA seal of approval could not be shown in an MPPDA movie theater.

Mae West, shown here in **She Done Him Wrong** *(1933), is famous for her humorous films with sexual overtones.*

In the film **Yes, My Darling Daughter,** *an unmarried couple* **(above)** *flirted through an open window of a cabin. Though the man slept on the porch, the film was banned because some groups felt young people who saw it would want to sleep together before marriage.*

Not everyone was pleased. The *New York Times* reported that many people booed the Production Code seal at the beginning of each movie.[13] Critics suggested that the Catholic Church was running the movie industry and that the use of censorship and boycotts was a threat to basic liberties.

From the early 1930s to the 1960s, no script was written or film produced that hadn't undergone thorough review by industry censors. Due to the enormous costs involved in producing a movie, studios shied away from anything controversial to avoid possible losses. Successful films consisted of simple moral tales. Real-life problems were either ignored or miraculously fixed.

By the mid-1960s, the situation had changed. Films reflected a society at odds over issues such as women's rights, the Vietnam War, and drugs. In 1968, in response to government pressure, the movie industry created a voluntary rating system. Films were assigned ratings of G (general audiences), M (mature audiences), R (restricted, under 16 not admitted without parent or guardian), and X (no one under 17 admitted). The M rating was later split into PG (parental guidance recommended) and PG-13, and the X rating became NC-17.

The rating system has not kept filmmakers from testing the limits of public acceptance. By the 1980s and 1990s, films contained more graphic sex and violence than ever before. Some audiences seemed to like it, but others thought filmmakers had gone too far.

HEAR NO EVIL

In the early 1970s, a New York man was shocked to hear comedian George Carlin's "Seven Dirty Words" sketch broadcast on the radio while he was driving with his young son in the car. The listener complained to the Federal Communications Commission (FCC), a government agency that regulates radio, wire, and cable communication. Although Carlin's language was offensive to some listeners, it did not meet the legal definition of obscenity. The FCC decided to recognize it as "indecency." The radio station fought the decision, and the case went all the way to the Supreme Court. FCC lawyers argued that an "indecency" standard could be used to prevent radio stations from broadcasting offensive material during the day, when children might be listening. The Supreme Court upheld the FCC's use of the indecency standard in broadcasting.[14]

In May 1985, Tipper Gore (wife of then Senator Al Gore) and her friend Susan Baker founded the Parents Music Resource Center (PMRC) to address the issue of song lyrics with sexual or Satanic content. The PMRC hoped to raise public awareness and begin a constructive dialogue with people in the entertainment industry. The issue of offensive song lyrics soon became a national issue. Columnist John Leo asked, "Why should our daughters have to grow up in a culture in which musical advice on the domination and abuse of women is accepted as entertainment?"[15]

By August, representatives of the record industry began to fight back, accusing the PMRC of promoting censorship. Musician Frank Zappa spoke against the

Tipper Gore, one of the founders of the Parents Music Resource Center (PMRC), has raised public awareness of graphic and offensive song lyrics.

Several rock groups' albums, including those of Marilyn Manson, carry parental warnings because of lyrics that, critics say, may be harmful to listeners.

PMRC plan before Congress. Zappa thought the PMRC proposal was "an ill-conceived piece of nonsense" that would not give any real benefits to children but would infringe on the civil liberties of adults. He compared the PMRC's demands to "treating dandruff by decapitation."[16]

Gore argued that her organization was attempting to *increase* information, not suppress it. They did not call for a ban on any album, no matter how offensive. Instead, the PMRC suggested that the use of labels warning about the lyrics be a visible part of the packaging of affected albums, tapes, and compact discs. Who would decide what was offensive and required warning labels? The PMRC said that the music industry itself should take that responsibility. As a result, selected albums have a warning that reads "Explicit Lyrics—Parental Advisory." The PMRC does not promote the restriction of sales to minors, but they do encourage parents to work with community leaders and retailers to develop the appropriate standards for their area.[17]

Music has often challenged authority, threatened social barriers, and created controversy. Should the government restrain that expression? Does the First Amendment protect even the most offensive lyrics?

X-rated movie theaters and lounges with live dancing can be found in major cities throughout the United States.

ART, AMUSEMENT, OR OBSCENITY?

In 1821, a Massachusetts court convicted Peter Holmes of publishing an obscene book when he reprinted John Cleland's novel *Fanny Hill: The Memoirs of a Woman of Pleasure.* (When this story about a prostitute had first been printed in England around 1740, a bookstore owner had been placed in the pillory for offering it for sale.) The judge thought the book was so obscene he wouldn't even let the jury see it, so Holmes was found guilty by 12 men who had never even read the book.[1]

WHAT IS OBSCENE?

"I know it when I see it," said U.S. Supreme Court Justice Potter Stewart. The justice was referring to obscenity during a 1964 case, *Jacobellis v. Ohio.* The *Jacobellis* case determined that part of the test for obscenity should be that the work in question is "utterly without redeeming social importance." This test was dropped, however, in 1973. While pornography can mean any sexually explicit material, obscenity is a legal concept with a specific definition. Material deemed obscene is not protected under the First Amendment.

Pornography is estimated to be a four-to-six-billion-dollar-a-year industry in the United States alone.[2] It can be in the form of photographs, videotapes, movies, magazines, and books. It is available through the mail, on-line, from vending machines, and in stores.

IS PORNOGRAPHY HARMFUL?

One of the reasons some people want to restrict pornography is that they are convinced it is harmful and contributes to violence. These people think pornography should be denied protection as free speech. For example, Donald E. Wildmon, president of the American Family Association said, "Our perspective is pornography is a destructive medium. It is not love, but sex and violence."[3] The U.S. Supreme Court *has* denied First Amendment protection in cases where there is a "clear and present danger of imminent lawless action," a test established in 1919 by Justice Oliver Wendell Holmes in *Schenck v. United States.* Many censorship opponents insist that such danger is neither clear nor present in pornographic materials.

In 1968, President Lyndon Johnson appointed the National Commission on Obscenity and Pornography to study whether pornography should be restricted. In 1970, the commission recommended to members of Congress that they "should not seek to interfere with the right of adults who wish to do so to read, obtain, or view explicit sexual materials." They based their decision on their conclusions that explicit sexual materials did no harm, that such materials are sought after by large numbers of people, that public opinion is against restraints, that the prohibitions are hard to enforce, and that it is unfair to limit adults to a level deemed suitable for children.

President Richard Nixon called the recommendations "morally bankrupt" and urged all the states to outlaw pornography. Congress seemed to agree, voting overwhelmingly to reject the recommendations.

In 1985, President Ronald Reagan established the Attorney General's Commission on Pornography, later called the Meese Commission after Attorney General Edwin Meese. This commission held hearings to review existing studies. Conservative religious crusaders, Donald Wildmon in particular, pushed for the inclusion of mainstream men's magazines, such as *Playboy* and *Penthouse*, in the broad category of pornography in the commission's report.

Before the report was published, a letter on Department of Justice letterhead was sent to a group of bookstore, drugstore, convenience store, and department store chains. The letter implied that the companies were suspected by the commission of distributing pornography and that if they didn't want to be identified in the final report, they should stop. A federal judge ordered the commission to retract its letter, but thousands of men's magazines and even some teen magazines, photography magazines, rock-and-roll magazines, and the swimsuit issue of *Sports Illustrated* were removed from stores.[4]

After an independent review found no link between sexually explicit materials and violent sex crimes, the commission asked Surgeon General C. Everett Koop to

Pornographic magazines are sold at many different types of stores.

collect still more information. Koop and the experts he consulted found that "children and adolescents who participate in the production of pornography experience adverse, enduring effects," but found no evidence that adult use of nonviolent pornography led to criminal behavior. Despite this, the *Final Report by the Attorney General's Commission on Pornography* stated that sexually violent material might increase the likelihood of male aggressive behavior toward women and that sexually explicit material might somehow lead to an increase in sexual violence. Henry E. Hudson, who chaired the commission, said they had used "common sense" in determining that pornography leads to violence. The commission did not recommend any new legislation but suggested that the existing laws should be enforced more aggressively.[5]

Some experts say it is the violence, not the sex, in pornography that can affect behavior. Edward Donnerstein, a social scientist at the University of California at Santa Barbara, measured aggressiveness in people shown violent, sexual images. He found that test subjects delivered more powerful simulated shocks after viewing violent, sexual images. "When we remove the sexual content from such films and just leave the aggressive content," says Donnerstein, "we find a similar pattern of aggression and asocial attitudes."[6]

Violent media can give violent people a "script" to follow. An FBI study of 36 serial killers found that 29 were attracted to pornography and used it in their sexual activity, which included rape-murder.[7] A 1985

The Attorney General's Commission on Pornography chairman Henry E. Hudson (right) presented the 2,000-page report to Attorney General Edwin Meese (left) in 1986.

survey, based on six years' experience with 2,380 sexual assault victims and offenders, estimated that 68 percent of the offenders beat or abused their victims after looking at pornographic material, and 58 percent showed pornography to their victims.[8] It is difficult to know if pornography actually inspired these unbalanced individuals to act.

Does pornography fuel the fantasies of violent individuals or are violent individuals drawn to pornography? Would eliminating pornography help prevent sex crimes? Is pornography, as one psychologist described it, "like a shot of whiskey to an alcoholic"?[9]

In an unbalanced person, anything can trigger violence. "I have seen rapes inspired by a particular piece of pornography and I have also seen mass murders inspired by *Time* magazine and suicides inspired by *The Deer Hunter* and violent crime inspired by R-rated films," said forensic psychiatrist Park Elliott Dietz.[10] Social worker Roland Johnson, who worked with adolescent rapists, said, "I don't think pornography has . . . much influence on those who rape. More important is what's happened to them in their past."[11]

Studies in other countries have found no link between pornography and violence. In some of the countries where pornography was legalized, rates of rape and sex offenses actually dropped, according to a Danish report. A study of rape in Denmark, Sweden, West Germany, and the United States found that the only country that experienced an increase in the number of rapes was the United States, the country with the strictest obscenity laws. Experts say this is because rape is a crime of violence, not sex.[12]

Could it be argued then that pornography is actually good for society? Many perfectly normal adults enjoy pornography. It may serve as a release, a harmless way to experience fantasies that could be hurtful if acted out in real life. Would crime increase if potentially violent individuals didn't have pornography as an outlet?

People who defend pornography generally do so on three basic grounds. First, all people are entitled to free expression. Second, this freedom cannot be restricted unless it results in harm to the interests of others. Third, pornography is a private transaction between a buyer and a seller.[13]

Critics argue that pornography does encourage, and even teach, unusual or illegal sexual acts. They feel that banning pornography would lead to fewer rapes, reduce the prevalence of incest, and decrease violence against women.

Catherine MacKinnon, professor of law at the University of Michigan Law School, and writer Andrea Dworkin are feminists who say that pornographic materials degrade and injure women. "The first victims of pornography are the ones in it," said MacKinnon. "The humiliating and abusive acts often depicted in pornographic films are actually happening to real women," she said. MacKinnon and Dworkin believe that pornography reinforces sexual inequality and promotes sexual violence against women.[14]

Some people want to do away with pornography whether or not it can be proven harmful. "There are lots of people who don't like this stuff and that is their constitutional right," said Marty Klein, a family counselor and sex therapist in Palo Alto, California. "But the intuitive belief that people have that pornography contributes to violence has not been proved. What people are saying is 'I feel bad that other people are watching this stuff and I want that to stop.'"[15]

FREEDOM FROM OR
FREEDOM FOR PORNOGRAPHY?

Censorship of materials due to sexual content is a relatively new idea. Materials that many Americans would consider pornographic were in common circulation in England for centuries. At the end of the sixteenth century, the Puritan view began to gain influence. The Puritans rejected all pleasure as sinful and immoral, but even they failed to define obscenity. They rarely attacked a work unless it was considered antireligious, and sexual materials circulated freely in the colonies.

Not until the mid- to late 1800s did the government begin to intervene in the censorship of obscene materials to any significant degree. In the early twentieth century, American courts used the standard of obscenity set by an English court in the 1868 case *Regina v. Hicklin*. The court defined obscenity as that which tended "to deprave and corrupt those whose minds are open to such immoral influences, and into whose hands a publication of this sort may fall." This definition came to be known as the Hicklin test. It was a landmark decision because it allowed, for the first time, the suppression of materials solely because of the sexual content, unrelated to any attack on religious or governmental institutions. Also, the determination of whether a book was obscene was based on isolated passages rather than on the work as a whole.

In 1933, the Hicklin test was rejected in *U.S. v. One Book Called Ulysses.* Judge John Woolsey said that in his opinion the preferred test should be based on the effect that the "entire book" would have on an "average person."[16]

In 1957, *Roth v. U.S.* upheld the constitutionality of the Comstock Law of 1873 but ruled that the Hicklin test unconstitutionally restricted the freedoms of speech and press. A work could no longer be judged obscene based on an isolated passage. The new obscenity test would be "whether to the average person,

Since its first publication in 1922, Ulysses *by James Joyce (right) has been repeatedly banned because of its explicit sexual content.*

applying contemporary community standards, the dominant theme of the material taken as a whole appeals to the prurient interest." Justice William J. Brennan Jr. stated that obscenity did not enjoy First Amendment protection because it is "utterly without redeeming social importance."[17]

In the 1973 case *Miller v. California,* the Supreme Court formulated a new legal definition of obscenity. The ruling instituted a three-part test:

1. The average person, applying contemporary community standards, would find that the work, taken as a whole, appeals to the prurient interest in sex.

2. The work depicts or describes sexual conduct in a patently offensive way.

3. The work, taken as a whole, lacks serious literary, artistic, political, or social value.

To be found obscene, the work had to meet all three criteria.[18]

Concern about child pornography led to the Protection of Children from Sexual Exploitation Act of 1977. The Act prohibited the production of any sexually explicit material using a child under the age of 16 if such material is destined for, or has already traveled in interstate commerce—commerce between one state and another. The Act forbade the transportation, shipping, mailing, or receipt of child pornography in interstate commerce for the purpose of sale or distribution for sale. It also required that the material pass the Miller test for obscenity. Violators were subject to penalties of 10 years in prison and/or a $10,000 fine.

The Child Protection Act of 1984 attempted to strengthen the 1977 law by dropping the Miller obscenity test, raising the age of the child to 18, eliminating the requirement that distribution be for the purpose of sale, and increasing the penalties.[19]

Pornography (including illegal, obscene materials) continues to be an enormous business, and the Internet has become an important distribution system. The originating source of on-line materials is harder to trace than that of print versions, and images can travel across continents quickly and anonymously. Nevertheless, over one hundred antiporn "cybercops," police who patrol the Internet, are trying to stop illegal activities. They made three hundred arrests in the first five months of 1997.[20]

Adult supervision of Internet use is the most common way of controlling the information children can access on-line.

CENSORSHIP GOES ON-LINE

It was a mother's nightmare. Her 13-year-old son was burned over 25 percent of his body when a bomb he was building exploded. What was a child doing with explosives? He was following directions he had found on the Internet. The mother decided to lobby for restrictions on what is available on-line.[1]

Almost as soon as the public began to use the Internet, people began to express concern about its use. Anyone with a computer could gain entry into sites all over the world. There were no restrictions on what (or who) could be on the Internet. Children could tap into information, pictures, videos, and conversations around the world. Suddenly young people could enter the adult world with the click of a mouse. No one can see them or know their age.

Many people find the diversity of sites on the Internet fascinating. Users can diagnose a "virtual patient," tour an art museum, listen to a new song, view a baseball play, or chat with a scientist in Antarctica. They can also meet people who want to have sex with children, learn how to make illegal drugs, read racist propaganda, or find out how to make a bomb from common household ingredients. The good, the bad, and the ugly are all easily accessible. That is the advantage—and the disadvantage—of the Internet.

PROTECTING THE CHILDREN

Almost anyone who has seen what is on the Internet would agree that some sites are not appropriate for children. But this position raises some questions. Should a child's access to the Internet be controlled? If so, who should determine what is appropriate for children? Can children's access be restricted without restricting access by adults?

Ginsburg v. New York made it a crime to sell materials defined as "harmful to minors" (but not obscene) to anyone under the age of 17. The Court asserted the power of the state to "protect" children, even if the exercise of that power meant an invasion of constitutionally protected freedoms. After the *Ginsburg* ruling, many states passed laws that banned not only the sale of sexually explicit materials to minors, but also the display of such materials if they would be accessible to minors. States tried to require "adults only" shelves or sections, but appellate courts have struck down these ordinances because they also restrict adult access to constitutionally protected materials. How do such rulings apply to the Internet?

Almost one-fourth of all people over 16 in the United States and Canada have access to the Internet.[2] In 1998, there were more than 100 million Web pages on the Internet, with tens of thousands being added every day. Experts estimate that about one percent of all Web pages contain material that could be considered offensive.[3] In addition to Web pages, the Internet has chat rooms, newsgroups, and listservs (sites that provide forums for unrestricted dialogue). These are used by an estimated 40 million people.[4]

The most effective way to control what a child accesses on the Internet would be for the parent to monitor the child's activities on the computer, but this arrangement is probably not feasible in many cases. For one thing, children can access the Internet from places other than home. In 1999, 85 percent of public schools and 73 percent of libraries in the United States provided Internet access.

Partly as a result of the concern about what is on the Internet, Congress passed the Telecommunications Act of 1996, which became known as the Communications Decency Act (CDA). It prohibited the posting of indecent or patently offensive material on a computer network to which minors have access, making it a crime with a maximum of two years in prison and $250,000 in fines.

The ACLU, libraries, publishers, and several other organizations challenged the CDA as unconstitutional on the grounds that it invaded privacy. The U.S. Supreme Court heard the case on March 19, 1997. Seth P. Waxman, the Deputy Solicitor General, said in his opening statement, "The Internet is a revolutionary advance in information technology. It also provides a revolutionary means for displaying patently offensive, sexually explicit material to children in the privacy of their homes." The justices raised questions to determine how the proposed law might work. Suppose groups of high school students were chatting about their sexual experiences on the Internet. Would they be guilty of a federal crime and subject to two years in prison? Is the Internet a private communication vehicle (like the telephone) or a public forum (like a street corner)?

The Court determined the CDA was unconstitutional and struck it down. The Court concluded that the Internet was like a vast library with content "as varied as human thought."[5] The ruling suggested that Internet-blocking software was a reasonably effective method available to parents wishing to restrict a child's access to potentially offensive material.

Internet-blocking programs restrict a child's access by filtering out sites that contain certain words, blocking chat room participation, or preventing access to the Internet entirely. Sixteen million people access the Internet through America Online, and millions more through Compuserve and other major on-line services that provide parental controls at no cost.[6]

Some Internet blocking programs have been criticized for filtering more than just vulgar words, nudity, and violence. Bennett Haselton, an 18-year-old college student, founded Peacefire, a youth alliance against Internet censorship that has 3,500 members, about half of whom are under 18. Haselton feels that a blocking program "infringes on the rights of children, parents, and teachers wherever the program is used."[7]

Haselton is particularly concerned that such programs block sites he considers perfectly appropriate for

kids but that may have political content. According to
Haselton, CYBERsitter, one of the most popular filtering programs, includes the Web site for the National
Organization for Women on its list of sites unsuitable
for children. Other sites blocked by filtering programs
he studied are Planned Parenthood, the Human Rights
Campaign, and the HIV/AIDS Information Center of
the American Medical Association. Brian Milburn,
president of Solid Oak Software, manufacturers of CY-
BERsitter, defends filtering software. "When your parents tell you what you can and cannot use, that is not
censorship," according to Milburn.[8] Haselton disagrees. He said, "Part of fighting censorship is urging
people to think for themselves, and you can't think
critically for yourself if you believe that your parents
are always right." He adds that long-held prejudices
will not change unless teens have the courage to think
differently from their parents.[9]

The Children's Internet Protection Act, proposed in
1999, would require public schools and libraries that
offer Internet access to children to use filtering programs on the computers children use. The ACLU has
challenged the law, claiming it violates the constitutional rights of both adults and minors.

A different way of restricting children's access to the
Internet would be to require a credit card number or
other adult identification in order to enter a site. This
idea was included in the Child Online Protection Act,
legislation designed to restrict children's access to the
Internet. President Bill Clinton signed the law in 1998,
but the ACLU challenged it, claiming it restricted freedom of speech.

Internet-blocking programs like Net Nanny (left) *and SURF-WATCH* (below) *restrict sites, chat room participation, or Internet access.*

Another possible solution is to restrict some sites to participants over a certain age. But screening out underage visitors in some areas—such as bulletin boards—can be difficult.

Parry Aftab is a cyberspace attorney and executive director of CyberAngels, an Internet-based organization that works to keep the Internet safe for children but opposes government regulation. She doesn't think that adults should be prohibited from viewing legal materials just because children might access them. She said, "I think there are less restrictive ways to control children's access. Many child advocacy groups believe that they are in the best position to tell adults what they should or shouldn't be reading on-line. In the United States, however, this doesn't fly. I wish that our legislators would understand that the First Amendment applies on-line as well as off-line."[10]

PRIVACY AND FREE SPEECH VERSUS CONTROL

When officials at Princeton University found that students and faculty were using their university e-mail or Web pages to send political messages, they decided to stop the practice. Although the university allowed the use of its system for personal communication, officials argued that such political activities could affect the university's status as a nonprofit institution. David Rocah, an ACLU lawyer, called the university's position "ridiculous." He said that, according to that logic, a professor using a university telephone "couldn't talk about who to vote for."[11]

Universities have also tried to restrict access to certain newsgroups (special-interest forums e-mail messages to those on the mailing list) because they consider them obscene. Many universities also screen student newspapers that are published on-line. Administrators believe that they, as publishers, have the responsibility to control what appears on university websites.

Libraries have struggled with whether—and to what extent—they have a responsibility to restrict Internet sites that are accessible from library computers. About 15 percent of libraries use filtering software to censor or filter Internet sites, even though the American Library Association opposes such restrictions.[12] While some people argue that libraries should not provide access to pornography, others compare Internet restrictions to book burning.

On-line services are concerned about their responsibilities, too. Could they be liable for failing to protect their subscribers from offensive, perhaps even dangerous, communications? Prodigy initially monitored all public postings, erasing those they considered offensive, such as those with racist or anti-Semitic content. (Users had signed a contract giving Prodigy the right to edit all public messages before they were posted.) Was this a valued service or an unwelcome, perhaps even illegal, restriction on the free exchange of thoughts and ideas?[13] America Online created a team of nearly 14,000 volunteers who patrol bulletin boards, looking for violations of its "terms of service." These terms require members to promise not to "harass, threaten, embarrass, or do anything else to another member that is unwanted."[14] In December 1998, managers at America Online suspended debate in the Irish Heritage discussion group when the conversations became heated. Both sides of the debate objected to the decision. One participant begged a member with an opposing point of view not to stop speaking out to appease the "AOL Thought Police," saying "I'd much rather have someone vehemently disagree with me than know that anyone has been silenced."[15]

Court cases are beginning to define what can and can't be restricted on the Internet. In 1999, an antiabortion website was fined $107 million for content considered threatening to abortion providers. The site listed physicians by name and included their home addresses, the names of their children, and their routes to work. It crossed off the names of doctors who had been killed and shaded those who had been wounded. The ACLU vowed to appeal the verdict, which the defendants termed a dangerous assault on free speech.

Many people are opposed to having their Internet activities scrutinized by the government or anyone else. Some sites are helpful to people specifically because individuals can be anonymous. Victims of abuse, people who have unusual sexual interests, and those trying to overcome addictions are among the Internet users who assume no one will know who they are. In reality, most sites keep logs of all visitors. It is also possible for individual sites to collect information such as e-mail address, type of computer, browser, general location, and even sites visited. Should Internet providers or the government be able to use this information to monitor on-line activities?

China, Singapore, and some other countries control Internet access of their citizens. China, for example, records every site accessed by its residents, making people think twice before visiting sites the government might frown upon.[16] In 1996, Chinese authorities listed one hundred foreign Internet sites that they had made inaccessible due to their alleged political or pornographic content. This list was later shortened, but in 1998, it appeared that Chinese censors had blocked Internet users in China from accessing the CNN and British Broadcasting Corporation websites, two of the world's most widely watched news sites.[17]

One of the complications in trying to restrict the content of the Internet is that it is a global medium. At least 40 percent of all content and 30 percent of indecent speech is posted from other countries.[18] The United States cannot control what is on the Internet anymore than a flea can control its dog. Any laws made by the U.S. government would affect only American Internet activities.

The Internet community, for the most part, has resisted attempts to censor cyberspace. A campaign for on-line intellectual freedom was established to raise

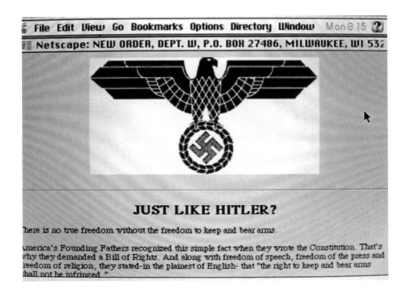

File Edit View Go Bookmarks Options Directory Window Mon 8 15

Netscape: NEW ORDER, DEPT. W, P.O. BOX 27486, MILWAUKEE, WI 53

JUST LIKE HITLER?

here is no true freedom without the freedom to keep and bear arms.

America's Founding Fathers recognized this simple fact when they wrote the Constitution. That's why they demanded a Bill of Rights. And along with freedom of speech, freedom of the press and freedom of religion, they stated-in the plainest of English- that "the right to keep and bear arms shall not be infringed."

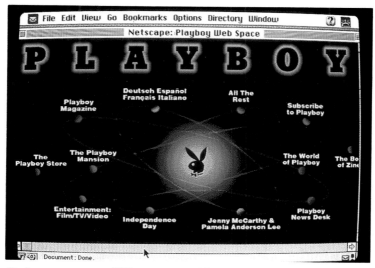

Only 15 percent of libraries use filtering software to censor Internet sites containing pornography (above) and messages that encourage the bearing of arms (facing page).

awareness of censorship in the electronic environment. Although the campaign fights for free speech as an essential human right, it specifically excludes sexual harassment, abuse of children, and "the breeding of hatred or intolerance." The campaign uses a folded blue ribbon (similar to the red AIDS-awareness ribbon) as its symbol.[19]

One country can probably do little to limit or control the Internet. Howard Rheingold, who writes about technology issues, speculates that the Internet—originally a "doomsday weapon" designed by the American military to allow communications even in the event of a nuclear attack—may actually create a new world in which people communicate openly about all sorts of subjects.[20]

THE·TRIAL·OF·JOHN·PETER·ZENGER·FOR·LIBEL
RESULTING·IN·THE·VICTORY·FOR·FREE·PRESS·AUG·4·1735

The 1735 trial of John Peter Zenger, publisher of the New York Weekly Journal, *resulted in a not-guilty verdict. Zenger had been accused of seditious libel against a British governor.*

WE'RE FROM THE GOVERNMENT, AND WE'RE HERE TO HELP YOU

In 1663, British subject William Twyn printed a book that endorsed the right of revolution. English authorities decided that Twyn had "compassed," or imagined, the death of the king. Twyn was given the standard punishment for treason. He was hanged, then cut down while still alive. His genitals were cut off, his belly was opened to spill out his internal organs, his arms and legs were pulled off, and finally, his head was cut off.[1]

Although we think of the early American colonists as freedom-loving people, they based their new government on a long history of English law, which had little concern for freedom of speech. Officials believed that criticizing the government could jeopardize security and lead to wars, revolutions, or other disastrous events. Speaking out against the government, a crime called seditious libel, was considered treason.

One of the first major victories for freedom of the press in the American colonies was won at the trial of

John Peter Zenger in 1735. Zenger, the printer, publisher, and editor of the *New York Weekly Journal,* had published several articles accusing the British governor, William Cosby, of influencing court cases, tampering with elections, and showing favoritism in making appointments. Zenger was arrested and tried for seditious libel.

Andrew Hamilton, a famous Philadelphia lawyer, went to New York to defend Zenger. Hamilton took quite an astonishing approach. He agreed that Zenger had printed the story, but Hamilton convinced the jury to find Zenger "not guilty" by arguing that Zenger had printed the truth, and that truth is not libelous. Hamilton explained that freedom of speech and of the press was essential to exposing government wrongdoing. Zenger was found not guilty, but the law remained unchanged.

Although American colonists wanted to protect their rights, they retained the law against seditious libel. In 1798, Congress passed the Sedition Act, which read in part, "If any person shall write, print, utter or publish . . . any false, scandalous and malicious writing or writings against the government . . . then such person . . . shall be punished by a fine not exceeding two thousand dollars, and by imprisonment not exceeding two years."[2] The law ended in 1801, but about a hundred years later, World War I and the fear of Communism led to its resurfacing.

LOOSE LIPS SINK SHIPS

During times of war, nations often restrict speech in an effort to suppress information that might benefit the enemy. During World War I, the Espionage Act of 1917 forbade the publication of information "related to national defense" and declared anyone who caused "insubordination in the Armed Forces" or interfered with the draft to be guilty of a felony. The act was later extended to include any "disloyal, profane, scurrilous, or abusive language about the form of government of the United States."[3]

During World War II (1939-1945), censors monitored letters that soldiers sent home, cutting out anything that could possibly give the enemy information. Even the traditional symbols for hugs and kisses—Xs and Os—were cut from letters because officials worried that the pattern could be a code explaining troop positions or ship movements.[4]

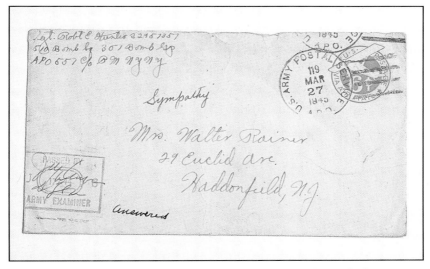

Fear of enemies obtaining secret information through the mail caused censors to cut out portions of letters in World War II and to pass them by an army examiner.

In 1971, the *New York Times* received a large number of classified documents from an anonymous
source. The documents, which came to be known as
the Pentagon Papers, revealed that the United States
had been waging a "secret war" in Vietnam. Editors at
the paper thought the public had a right to know the
situation. On June 13, 1971, the *New York Times* published the first installment of the 18-volume document.
The following day, Attorney General John Mitchell, at
the request of President Richard Nixon, asked the
newspaper to return the documents and to stop publishing them. The *Times* refused. The case went to
court, and the Supreme Court upheld the newspaper's
right to publish the highly secret and sensitive documents.[5]

As recently as the 1991 Gulf War, sometimes called
Operation Desert Storm, the U.S. government restricted
information available to the media. The war was fought
between Iraq and a coalition of 39 countries organized
mainly by the United States and the United Nations in
response to Iraq's invasion of Kuwait. During the war,
U. S. officials restricted where reporters could go and
what they could report. The Freedom of Information
Act allows Americans access to more information than
in the past, but the government can still withhold certain kinds of information, especially if it is related to
national security.

GOVERNMENT CENSORSHIP AROUND THE WORLD
In some countries, the government routinely silences
criticism by imposing censorship. The Indonesian government, for example, has banned nearly two thousand

books, jailed authors and journalists, and intimidated publishers and booksellers. Wendy Wolf, an editor at Penguin USA who chaired the Association of American Publishers delegation to Indonesia, said that the Indonesian government has created a "culture of fear" and has jailed people just for having a banned book in their possession.[6]

In 1997, the congress in Colombia, the fourth largest country in South America, gave a regulatory agency the authority to cancel television news programs based on their content. Many journalists think the agency punishes programs that investigate ties between government officials and drug dealers.[7]

South African author J. M. Coetzee distrusts censorship. "The institution of censorship puts power into the hands of persons with a judgmental, bureaucratic cast of mind that is bad for the cultural and even the spiritual life of the community," he says.[8] From the early 1960s until about 1980, censorship was widely practiced in South Africa. A "publications control" system monitored not only books and films but also T-shirts, toys, key rings, store signs—anything that could possibly carry a message the government would find offensive.

One of the most famous cases in recent years is that of British writer Salman Rushdie. Rushdie's 1989 book, *The Satanic Verses,* angered Islamic fundamentalists. They thought the book insulted their religion. In a radio broadcast, the Ayatollah Ruhollah Khomeini of Iran declared: "I inform the proud Muslim people of the world that the author of *The Satanic Verses,* which is against Islam, the Prophet, and the Koran, and all

Salman Rushdie holds up his controversial book The Satanic
Verses. *The Ayatollah Khomeini of Iran accused Rushdie of
insulting the Islamic religion and called for the author's
death.*

those involved in its publication who were aware of its
contents, are sentenced to death."[9] A militant organization in Iran offered a reward for killing Rushdie, and
the author was forced into hiding. But Rushdie wasn't
the only one targeted. Bombs were placed outside
bookstores in England, the Japanese translator for the
book was murdered, the Italian translator was stabbed,
and the director of a publishing house in Norway was
shot. Scores of protesters were killed or injured, and
booksellers around the world were intimidated.

When Rushdie came out of hiding after the Iranian
government lifted the official death threat in 1998, he
commented that he had no regrets about writing the
book and said, among other things, that the fight was
over "the overarching issue of free speech."[10]

Egypt's cultural life is the most Westernized in the Arab world, making it a target for militant Islamic fundamentalists seeking to prevent public exposure to Western images and ideas the extremists believe to be in conflict with Islamic laws and beliefs. They use the courts to protect "God's rights" by suppressing Western influences and to ban books, movies, and articles not in accordance with fundamentalist Islamic views.[11] In China, a popular magazine was shut down in 1999 as part of a crackdown on publications that criticize the government or express views that conflict with official policies.

Ken Saro-Wiwa, a Nigerian writer who was hanged by his government for his writing and protest activities, said before his death, "The men who ordain and supervise this show of shame, this tragic charade, are frightened by the word, the power of ideas, the power of the pen, by the demands of social justice and the rights of man. Nor do they have a sense of history. They are so scared of the power of the word, that they do not read. And that is their funeral."[12]

Journalists may be threatened, imprisoned, exiled, or even killed for writing stories that expose organized crime, atrocities of war, or corrupt officials. Killing the story by killing the reporter may be the ultimate form of censorship. According to an annual report by Reporters without Borders and the Committee to Protect Journalists, 26 journalists were killed on the job in various parts of the world in 1997, and at least 129 journalists were being held in 24 countries. The countries with the highest numbers of jailed journalists were Turkey (29), Nigeria (17), Ethiopia (16), and China (15).

Ken Saro-Wiwa was hanged in Nigeria for his writing and protest activities.

Sixty journalists have been assassinated in Algeria since 1993 while reporting on the civil war, which was triggered when army-backed authorities canceled a 1992 election that Islamic militants were expected to win.[13]

Journalists in Mexico, Colombia, and other Latin American countries have been killed for reporting on drug trafficking and government corruption. For example, in 1997, an Argentinian photographer was shot and burned while working on a story that involved suspected government corruption.[14] The report stated, "Murdering a journalist in order to silence him remains too current a practice around the world."[15]

GOVERNMENT FUNDING FOR THE ARTS
Government funding for the arts in the United States, largely through the National Endowment for the Arts, assists individuals and nonprofit organizations in a

wide range of artistic endeavors. Additional funds aid activities in the arts that are sponsored by the states. Such funding brings cultural events to schools, supports musical groups, helps fund local art agencies, and provides a way for struggling artists to survive. The tradition of providing assistance to the arts dates back centuries and is shared by most developed countries. Many Americans, however, have become reluctant to fund art they find offensive or don't understand.

Robert Mapplethorpe was considered one of the foremost photographers in the United States. His subjects included flowers, portraits, and the human body. In June 1989, the Corcoran Gallery of Art in Washington, D.C., canceled its scheduled exhibit of Mapplethorpe's photographs of gay men in erotic poses.

Jesse Helms, a conservative senator from North Carolina, was appalled when he learned that the Mapplethorpe exhibit had been funded by the National Endowment for the Arts. Helms said, "There's a big difference between *The Merchant of Venice* and a photograph of two males of different races on a marble table top. . . . The Mapplethorpe fellow was an acknowledged homosexual . . . the theme goes throughout his work."[16] Mapplethorpe, who died in 1989, explained that "my intent was to open people's eyes, to realize anything can be acceptable. It's not what it is, it's the way that it's photographed."[17]

Some people saw the issue as freedom *from* expression—and freedom of Americans from subsidizing art projects of which they don't approve. "This matter does not involve freedom of expression," said Alphonse D'Amato, then senator from New York. "It does involve

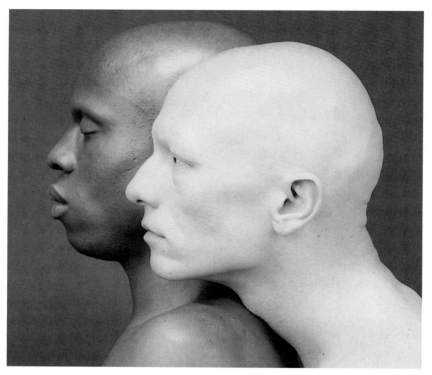

In June 1989, Robert Mapplethorpe's photographs of homosexual men of different races were criticized when they were exhibited at the Washington Project for the Arts in Washington, D.C.

the question whether American taxpayers should be forced to support such trash."[18]

Should the government pay for art that offends some taxpayers? Former president George Bush said in 1990, "I am deeply offended by some of the filth that I see and to which federal money has gone, and some of the sacrilegious, blasphemous depictions that are portrayed by some to be art . . . [which] has no business of getting one cent of taxpayers' money."[19]

Journalist David S. Broder disagrees. In a 1992 article for the *Washington Post,* he compared the unwillingness of some people to have their tax dollars go to controversial works of art to his own aversion to having his taxes pay for soldiers who kill other soldiers with "friendly fire" or police officers who abuse suspects. He doesn't like it, but he doesn't advocate abolishing the military or the police department. Bureaucracies make mistakes, he says, "but a nation that cannot afford to finance its arts—even the occasionally tasteless or offensive variety—is a nation that has lost its perspective, its self-confidence and probably its soul."[20] Already the United States spends less on federal support of the arts—less than one dollar per person—than any other Western nation.

What kind of art would everyone approve of? How would that be determined? Is there a place for art that offends? What if it insults someone's religion, mocks traditional values, or promotes alternative lifestyles? When John Frohnmayer was forced to resign as chairman of the National Endowment for the Arts in 1992, he told his staff, "I leave with the belief that this eclipse of the soul will soon pass and with it the lunacy that sees artists as enemies and ideas as demons."[21]

Demonstrators in the United States protested censorship of the press's coverage of the Gulf War in 1991.

WHAT THE
FUTURE HOLDS

In the case involving Steven Pico's claim that the school board had deprived him of his First Amendment rights by removing certain books from his school's library, the court initially ruled in favor of the school board. The case was appealed and eventually reached the U.S. Supreme Court in 1982.

The Court ruled 5 to 4 in favor of Pico but decided that the case should have been tried to determine the board's motivation for removing the books. Justice William Brennan concluded that "the First Amendment imposes limitations upon a local school board's exercise of its discretion to remove books from high school and junior high school libraries." He continued, "Petitioners possess significant discretion to determine the content of their school libraries, but that discretion may not be exercised in a narrowly partisan or political manner. Whether petitioners' removal of books from the libraries denied respondents their First Amendment rights depends upon the motivation behind petitioners' actions. Local school boards may not

Steven Pico (left) *with attorneys Alan H. Levine* (center) *and Art Eisenberg* (right) *in 1982. The Supreme Court supported Pico's claim that the removal of certain books from school libraries is a form of censorship.*

remove books from school libraries simply because they dislike the ideas contained in those books and seek by their removal to 'prescribe what shall be orthodox in politics, nationalism, religion, or other matters of opinion.'"[1]

The school board declined to pursue the case further, and the books were returned. When Pico looks back, he is amazed that such a small group of people was able to keep books off the school shelves for the seven years the case took to settle. "Not one teacher, not one student, ever objected to these books," he says. Only one teacher ever even mentioned the case to him. "Steve, you're doing the right thing," she whispered to him one day after class. "I will never be able to forget that she felt the need to whisper," recalls Pico.[2]

The censorship issue affects many different types of expression—hate speech, art funded by government money, commercial advertising, pornography, Internet communications, school materials, entertainment media, and news reporting. A wide variety of special interest groups advocate censorship as part of their political or religious agendas. Social conflicts such as racial tensions and fear of new technological advancements have added to the confusion. Problems arise when the right to freedom of expression conflicts with other rights.

PROTECTING US FROM OURSELVES

Are differing points of view so dangerous? If fundamentalist Christian children learn about evolution, will they lose their religious convictions? If teenagers see an ad for a birth control device, will they decide to have sex? If adults view a pornographic movie, will they be inspired to rape and murder? Does diversity enrich or diminish our lives? Is knowledge valuable or dangerous?

Adults have a responsibility to protect children. Parents who abuse or neglect their children can be arrested and jailed. Are they also obligated to prevent children from seeing or hearing something inappropriate for their age? Should the government require that those who make and sell sensitive materials also help protect children?

TV personality Bob Keeshan (Captain Kangaroo) said that parents have to guide children in their choices. Parents can't just turn their responsibility over to others. "We would never think of calling the police and saying, 'I'm sending my child out to play. Stop all traffic!' You assume the responsibility of training your child to stay out of the street and out of harm's way."[3]

Jon Katz, author of *The Rights of Kids in the Digital Age,* thinks that censoring and blocking should be the last resort, not the first, particularly if children have been given the moral foundation and sense of responsibility required to handle mature material.[4]

America is known as a nation of free speakers, yet according to Patrick Garry, an author who studies media and First Amendment issues, American behavior contradicts that image. "Given the American love of and fascination with speech," says Garry, "the underlying cause of all censorship attempts does not appear to be an antispeech attitude prevalent in society. Instead, censorship attempts may result from a fear of the destructive power of certain speech and reflect a desperate move to release society from being a hostage to such speech."[5] Although most people would say they favor free speech, many are afraid of some kinds of speech and want restrictions to protect society from what they see as a threat.

INTO THE NEW MILLENNIUM

Changes in technology and the growing role of business in society may increasingly affect what is available to the public through the media in the future. The trend toward small publishers being bought by large conglomerates may bring about a return to the days when a few people controlled what the public read. In 1976, the United States had 50 major publishing companies. By 1998, that number had dropped to four.[6]

Bob Keeshan ("Captain Kangaroo") supported a Senate bill aimed at limiting children's exposure to violence on television.

The same thing is happening in the telecommunications industry as computer giants, telephone companies, cable operators, and new technologies such as Web TV begin to consolidate.

As magazines tighten their focus to appeal to more and more specialized groups, the pool of promising advertisers narrows. Potentially, this situation can give advertisers power over editorial content. Betsy Frank, executive vice president of Zenith Media Services, a company that buys advertising for clients, says, "If an advertiser is spending millions of dollars on TV advertising, or to appear in a magazine, they're not spending that money to support a free press, but as a business decision."[7]

The flow of ideas and access to information have been changed by corporate culture. In the future, pressure in the marketplace could increasingly affect freedom of expression—a store refuses to sell, a library decides not to buy, a sponsor declines to advertise. As

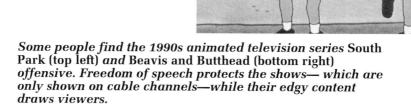

Some people find the 1990s animated television series South Park *(top left)* and *Beavis and Butthead (bottom right) offensive. Freedom of speech protects the shows— which are only shown on cable channels—while their edgy content draws viewers.*

huge corporations under the direction of a few powerful people control greater and greater parts of our society, free expression may suffer.

As a free society, we will have to continue to struggle with censorship issues, and the ramifications can be great. Joan Hoff-Wilson is a historian who contributed to a book on censorship produced by the New York Public Library in 1984. Hoff-Wilson questioned whether censorship was merely the first step along the way to losing other freedoms. She wrote, "Once we have accepted interlocking local and federal censorship of speech, information, and actions, can we long avoid losing other civil liberties in the name of secrecy and security?"[8]

While some would say such fears are unfounded, only the future will tell.

Resources to Contact

American Civil Liberties Union
132 West 43rd Street
New York, NY 10036
<http://www.aclu.org>

American Family Association
P. O. Drawer 2440
Tupelo, MS 38803
601-844-5036
<http://www.afa.net>

American Library Association
   Office for Intellectual Freedom
50 East Huron Street
Chicago, IL 60611
1-800-545-2433, ext. 4223
<http://www.ala.org>

Blue Ribbon Campaign
<http://www.eff.org/
blueribbon.html>

Cyberangels
<http://www.cyberangels.org>

Family Friendly Libraries
7597 Whisperwood Court
Springfield, VA 22153
703-440-9419
<http://www.fflibraries.org>

Morality in Media
475 Riverside Drive
New York, NY 10115
212-870-3222
<http://pw2.netcom.com/~mimnyc/
index.html>

National Coalition Against
   Censorship
132 West 43rd Street
New York, NY 10036
<http://www.ncac.org>

National Coalition for the Protection
of Children and Families
800 Compton Road
Suite 9224
Cincinnati, OH 45231
513-521-6227

People for the American Way
2000 M Street NW
Washington, DC 20036
<http://www.pfaw.org>

Student Press Law Center
1815 North Fort Myer Drive
Suite 900
Arlington, VA 22209-1817
703-807-1904
<http://www.splc.org>

Endnotes

CHAPTER 1. THE CENSORSHIP ISSUE

[1]Herbert N. Foerstel, *Banned in the U.S.A.: A Reference Guide to Book Censorship in Schools and Public Libraries* (Westport, Conn.: Greenwood Press, 1994), 13–14.

[2]George Beahm, ed., *War of Words: The Censorship Debate* (Kansas City, Mo.: Andrews and McMeel, 1993), 326.

[3]"AIDS Campaign Dropped as Religion and Advertising Clash," *New York Times*, February 24, 1997.

[4]Joan Del Fattore, *What Johnny Shouldn't Read* (New Haven Conn.: Yale University Press, 1992), 13.

[5]Tom Blair, "Censorship at The Pottstown Mercury," <http://www.stormfront.org/>, 1997.

[6]Nat Hentoff, *Free Speech for Me—But Not for Thee: How the American Left and Right Relentlessly Censor Each Other* (New York: HarperCollins, 1992), 265.

[7]Cesar G. Soriano, "Greaseman Tries to Clear the Air," *USA Today,* March 4, 1999.

[8]Lee Bennett Hopkins, "Shut Not Your Doors: An Author Looks at Censorship," *Censored Books: Critical Viewpoints,* eds. Nicholas J. Karolides, Lee Burress, and John M. Kean (Metuchen, N. J.: The Scarecrow Press, Inc., 1993), 45

[9]Ibid., 44.

CHAPTER 2. CENSORSHIP THROUGHOUT HISTORY

[1]Paul S. Boyer, *Purity in Print: The Vice-Society Movement and Book Censorship in America* (New York: Charles Scribner's Sons, 1968), 269.

[2]Ibid.

[3]Jane Clapp, *Art Censorship: A Chronology of Proscribed and Prescribed Art* (Metuchen, N. J.: The Scarecrow Press, Inc., 1972), 23.

[4]Michael R. Collings, "Censorship in the Renaissance: A Paradigm for Today?" *War of Words: The Censorship Debate,* ed. George Beahm (Kansas City, Mo.: Andrews and McMeel, 1993), 10.

[5]Ibid., 13.

[6]Joel H. Wiener, "Social Purity and Freedom of Expression," *Censorship: 500 Years of Conflict,* New York Public Library, ed. (New York: Oxford University Press, 1984), 96.

[7]Steven C. Dubin, *Arresting Images: Impolitic Art and Uncivil Actions* (New York: Routledge, 1992), 237.

[8]Wiener, 101.

[9]Boyer, 21.

[10]William Noble, *Bookbanning in America: Who Bans Books?—And Why?* (Middlebury, Vt.: Paul S. Eriksson, 1990), 100.

[11]Boyer, 23.

[12]Ibid., 17.

[13]Ibid., 93.

[14]Ibid., 122.

[15]Ibid., 145.

[16]Ibid., 211.

[17]Ibid., 247.

CHAPTER 3. CENSORSHIP GOES TO SCHOOL

[1]"Student's Fight for Decency Denounced as Censorship," *Education Reporter,* February 1994, 1, 3.

[2]Clapp, 320–321.

[3]Judie Glave, "*Nappy* Author Defends Teacher Removed from Class," AP Online, November 25, 1998.

[4]"Evolution Controversy Boils Up in Kentucky," <http://dailynews.yahoo.com/h/nm/19991005/pl/evolution_Kentucky_1.html>, (October 5, 1999).

[5]Arthur J. Kropp, "Using Parents as a Trojan Horse for School Censorship," *War of Words: The Censorship Debate,* 190.

[6]Foerstel, 156.

[7]Zibby Oneal, "They Tell You to Do Your Own Thing, but They Don't Mean It: Censorship and *The Chocolate War,*" *Censored Books: Critical Viewpoints,* 183.

[8]Mark I. West, *Trust Your Children: Voices against Censorship in Children's Literature* (New York: Neal-Schuman Publishers, 1988), 10–12.

[9]Hopkins, 46.

[10]Stephen Bates, *Battleground: One Mother's Crusade, the Religious Right, and the Struggle for Control of Our Classrooms* (New York: Poseidon Press, 1993), 27.

[11]Greg R. Jesson, "How Parents Can Refute the 'Censor' Label," *War of Words: The Censorship Debate,* 181–182.

[12]Hentoff, 358.

[13]Goodman, Mark, telephone interview by author, 1997.

[14]John Leo, "Don't Steal This Column!" *U.S. News & World Report,* March 3, 1997, 19.

CHAPTER 4. AN EYE ON THE ENTERTAINMENT MEDIA

[1]"Girl, 8, Is Killed as Playmates Imitate Film's Shooting Scene," *New York Times,* February 13, 1997.

[2]Thomas Johnson, "The Decline of Television's Family Hour," *USA Today,* November 1996.

[3]Cheryl Wetzstein, "Sex Stars in Many TV Shows," *Washington Times,* February 10, 1999.

[4]Lawrie Mifflin, "TV Rating System May Actually Lure Youths to Violent Shows, Study Finds," *New York Times,* March 27, 1997.

[5]Jube Shiver Jr., "Study Finds Underuse of TV Ratings; Television: When Sexual or Violent Fare Is Shown, Content-Based Designations Are Not Being Widely Employed, Researchers Claim, but Others Fault Its Methodology," *Los Angeles Times,* September 25, 1998.

[6]Frank Walsh, *Sin and Censorship: The Catholic Church and the Motion Picture Industry* (New Haven, Conn.: Yale University Press, 1996), 6.

[7]Gregory D. Black, *Hollywood Censored: Morality Codes, Catholics, and the Movies* (Cambridge, England: Cambridge University Press, 1994), 5.

[8]Walsh, 7.

[9]Black, 32.

[10]Ibid.

[11]Walsh, 34.

[12]Ibid., 97.

[13]Ibid., 110.

[14]Susan Benkelman, "Day in Court for Internet," *Newsday,* March 18, 1997.

[15]Edward De Grazia, *Girls Lean Back Everywhere: The Law of Obscenity and the Assault on Genius* (New York: Random House, 1992), 657–658.

[16]Frank Zappa, "Mythical Beasts," *War of Words: The Censorship Debate,* 279.

[17]Parents Music Resource Center, "A Brief Overview of Explicit Lyrics and State Legislation," *War of Words: The Censorship Debate,* 273.

CHAPTER 5. ART, AMUSEMENT, OR OBSCENITY?

[1]Melvin Berger, *Censorship* (New York: Franklin Watts, 1982), 15.

[2]Franklin Mark Osanka and Sara Lee Johann, *Sourcebook on Pornography* (Lexington, Mass.: Lexington Books, 1989), 15.

[3]Wendy Melillo, "Can Pornography Lead to Violence?" *War of Words: The Censorship Debate,* 302.

[4]De Grazia, 600.

[5]Ibid., 606.

[6]Melillo, 304.

[7]Osanka and Johann, 81.

[8]Ibid.

[9]Ibid.

[10]Melillo, 304.

[11]Hentoff, 347.

[12]Melillo, 305.

[13]J. M. Coetzee, *Giving Offense: Essays on Censorship* (Chicago: University of Chicago Press, 1996), 21.

[14]De Grazia, 587.

[15]Melillo, 302.

[16]Margaret C. Jasper, "The Law of Obscenity and Pornography," *Oceana's Legal Almanac Series: Law for the Layperson* (Dobbs Ferry, N. Y.: Oceana Publications, Inc., 1996), 4.

[17]Berger, 16.

[18]Jasper, 6.

[19]Ibid.

[20]David E. Kaplan "New Cybercop Tricks to Fight Child Porn: Police Struggle against an On-line Onslaught," *U.S. News & World Report,* May 26, 1997, 29.

CHAPTER 6. CENSORSHIP GOES ON-LINE

[1]Cheryl White and Heather Moors Johnson, "My Son Built a Bomb," *Ladies Home Journal,* March 1997, 36–38.

[2]Benkelman, A4, A30.

[3]Christopher J. Portelli and Coralie W. Meade, "Censorship and the Internet—

No Easy Answers," *Contemporary Women's Issues Database,* October 1, 1998, 4–8.

⁴"Transcripts of Supreme Court, Janet Reno, *Attorney General of the United States et al. v. American Civil Liberties Union,* No. 96–511, March 19, 1997," <http://www.aclu.org/issues/cyber/trial/sctran.html> (1997).

⁵Ibid.

⁶Susan Aschoff, "A Parental Challenge: Surfing the Internet," *Washington Times,* March 2, 1999.

⁷Pamela Mendels, "Youth Group Takes on Site-Filtering Software," *New York Times on the Web,* December 28, 1996.

⁸Ibid.

⁹Bennett Haselton, personal communication by author, March 18, 1999.

¹⁰Parry Aftab, personal communication by author, March 29, 1999.

¹¹Brian Doherty, "Internet Responsibility," *Reason*, February 1997, 13.

¹²Curtis Howell, "Libraries Face Tough Choices on Net Filters: Plano Case Illustrates Debate on Open Access, Censorship," *Dallas Morning News,* November 14, 1998.

¹³Howard Rheingold, *The Virtual Community: Homesteading on the Electronic Frontier* (Reading, Mass.: Addison-Wesley Publishing Company, 1993), 277–278.

¹⁴Amy Harmon, "Worries about Big Brother at America Online," *New York Times,* January 31, 1999.

¹⁵Ibid., 1.

¹⁶Simon Fluendy, "Can the Net Be Censored?" *World Press Review,* January 1997, 46.

¹⁷Joseph Albright, "China May Have Blocked Web Sites of CNN, BBC: Net-Savvy Users Have No Problems Foiling Censors," *Atlanta Journal and Constitution,* October 17, 1998.

¹⁸Ibid.

¹⁹"Blue Ribbon Campaign," <http://www.eff.org/blueribbon.html,> (1997).

²⁰Rheingold, 14–15.

CHAPTER 7. WE'RE FROM THE GOVERNMENT, AND WE'RE HERE TO HELP YOU

¹Leonard W. Levy, *Legacy of Suppression: Freedom of Speech and Press in Early American History* (Cambridge, Mass.: The Belknap Press of Harvard University, 1960), 11.

²Berger, 31.

³Ibid., 31–32.

⁴William Gass, "Shears of the Censor," *Harper's,* April 1997, 59.

⁵D. J. Herda, *New York Times v. United States: National Security and Censorship, Landmark Supreme Court Cases* (Hillside, N. J.: Enslow Publishers, Inc., 1994), n.p.

⁶Calvin Reid and Bridget Kinsella, "In Banned Books Week, Censorship Still Thrives," *Publishers Weekly,* September 23, 1996, 12.

⁷Diana Jean Schemo, "New TV Law in Columbia Provokes Complaints of Censorship," *New York Times,* February 3, 1997, 4.

⁸Coetzee, 9–10.

[9]Beahm, 57.

[10]Marjorie Miller, "Joyful Rushdie Steps Out of Shadows; Religion: Lifting of Iranian Death Threat Buoys Author of *Satanic Verses*: He Remains Cautious, but Says He Feels Free," *Los Angeles Times,* September 26, 1998, A1.

[11]Alan Cooperman, "First Bombs, Now Lawsuits: Egypt's Vibrant Cultural Life Is the Target of a New Legal Assault by Islamic Fundamentalists," *U.S. News & World Report,* December 23, 1996, 38.

[12]Gass, 65.

[13]Donna Abu-Nasr, "Twenty-Six Journalists Killed Worldwide Last Year," UPI Online, March 26, 1998.

[14]James Anderson, "Journalism Is a Dangerous, Sometimes Deadly Profession, Press Meeting Told," AP Online, March 15, 1998.

[15]"Journalist Toll in '97 Down to 26, Groups Say," *New York Times,* January 9, 1998.

[16]De Grazia, 622.

[17]Ibid., 626.

[18]Ibid., 627.

[19]Beahm, 73.

[20]Ibid., 88.

[21]Ibid., 118.

CHAPTER 8. WHAT THE FUTURE HOLDS

[1]<http://caselaw.findlaw.com/scripts/getcase.pl?navby=case&court=US&vol=457&page=853>.

[2]Foerstel, 13–14.

[3]Gary L. Wood, "The Censorship Game Hype in Hollywood," *War of Words: The Censorship Debate,* 235.

[4]Jon Katz, "The Rights of Kids in the Digital Age," *Wired,* July 1996, 120-123.

[5]Patrick Garry, *An American Paradox: Censorship in a Nation of Free Speech* (Westport, Conn.: Praeger, 1993), 11.

[6]Ray Suarez, "Book Industry Mergers," *Talk of the Nation,* National Public Radio, June 2, 1998.

[7]Paul D. Colford, "Pressured to Please: Advertiser's Concerns about Story Content Are Having an Impact on Magazine Editors," *Newsday,* May 28, 1997.

[8]Joan Hoff-Wilson, "The Pluralist Society," *Censorship: 500 Years of Conflict,* 115.

Bibliography

"AIDS Campaign Dropped as Religion and Advertising Clash." *The New York Times,* February 24, 1997.

Bates, Stephen. *Battleground: One Mother's Crusade, the Religious Right, and the Struggle for Control of Our Classrooms.* New York: Poseidon Press, 1993.

Beahm, George, ed. *War of Words: The Censorship Debate.* Kansas City, Mo.: Andrews and McMeel, 1993.

Berger, Melvin. *Censorship.* New York: Franklin Watts, 1982.

Black, Gregory D. *Hollywood Censored: Morality Codes, Catholics, and the Movies.* Cambridge, England: Cambridge University Press, 1994.

"Blue Ribbon Campaign." <http://www.eff.org/blueribbon.html> (1997).

Boyer, Paul S. *Purity in Print: The Vice-Society Movement and Book Censorship in America.* New York: Charles Scribner's Sons, 1968.

"Censored: The Campaign against the Media." *Mother Jones,* May/June 1996.

Clapp, Jane. *Art Censorship: A Chronology of Proscribed and Prescribed Art.* Metuchen, N.J.: The Scarecrow Press, Inc., 1972.

Coetzee, J. M. *Giving Offense: Essays on Censorship.* Chicago: University of Chicago Press, 1996.

Colford, Paul D. "Pressured to Please: Advertisers' Concerns about Story Content Are Having an Impact on Magazine Editors." *Newsday,* May 28, 1997.

Cooperman, Alan. "First Bombs, Now Lawsuits: Egypt's Vibrant Cultural Life Is the Target of a New Legal Assault by Islamic Fundamentalists." *U.S. News & World Report,* December 23, 1996.

Cozic, Charles P., ed. *Civil Liberties.* San Diego, Calif.: Greenhaven Press, 1994.

De Grazia, Edward. *Girls Lean Back Everywhere: The Law of Obscenity and the Assault on Genius.* New York: Random House, 1992.

Del Fattore, Joan. *What Johnny Shouldn't Read.* New Haven, Conn.: Yale University Press, 1992.

Doherty, Brian. "Internet Responsibility." *Reason,* February 1997.

Dubin, Steven C. *Arresting Images: Impolitic Art and Uncivil Actions.* New York: Routledge, 1992.

Fluendy, Simon. "Can the Net Be Censored?" *World Press Review,* January 1997.

Foerstel, Herbert N. *Banned in the U.S.A.: A Reference Guide to Book Censorship in Schools and Public Libraries.* Westport, Conn.: Greenwood Press, 1994.

Garry, Patrick. *An American Paradox: Censorship in a Nation of Free Speech.* Westport, Conn.: Praeger, 1993.

Gass, William. "Shears of the Censor." *Harper's,* April 1997.

"Girl, 8, Is Killed as Playmates Imitate Film's Shooting Scene." *New York Times,* February 13, 1997.

Hentoff, Nat. *Free Speech for Me—But Not for Thee: How the American Left and Right Relentlessly Censor Each Other.* New York: HarperCollins, 1992.

Herda, D. J. *New York Times v. United States: National Security and Censorship, Landmark Supreme Court Cases.* Springfield, N.J.: Enslow Publishers, Inc., 1994.

"Is Your Kid Caught Up in the Web? How to Find the Best Parts—and Avoid the Others." *Consumer Reports,* May 1997.

Jasper, Margaret C. "The Law of Obscenity and Pornography." *Oceana's Legal Almanac Series: Law for the Layperson.* Dobbs Ferry, N.Y.: Oceana Publications, Inc., 1996.

Johnson, Thomas. "The Decline of Television's Family Hour." *USA Today,* November 1996.

Kaplan, David E. "New Cybercop Tricks to Fight Child Porn: Police Struggle Against an On-line Onslaught." *U.S. News & World Report,* May 26, 1997.

Karolides, Nicholas J., Lee Burress, and John M. Kean, eds. *Censored Books: Critical Viewpoints.* Metuchen, N.J.: The Scarecrow Press, 1993.

Katz, Jon. "The Rights of Kids in the Digital Age." *Wired,* July 1996.

Lang, Susan S., and Paul Lang. *Censorship.* New York: Franklin Watts, 1993.

Leo, John. "Don't Steal This Column!" *U.S. News & World Report,* March 3, 1997.

Leone, Bruno, ed. *Free Speech.* San Diego: Greenhaven Press, Inc., 1994.

Levy, Leonard W. *Legacy of Suppression: Freedom of Speech and Press in Early American History.* Cambridge, Mass.: The Belknap Press of Harvard University, 1960.

Marsh, Dave. *50 Ways to Fight Censorship and Important Facts to Know about the Censors.* New York: Thunder's Mouth Press, 1991.

Mifflin, Lawrie. "Objections to Ratings." *New York Times.* April 9, 1997.

_____. "TV Rating System May Actually Lure Youths to Violent Shows, Study Finds." *New York Times,* March 27, 1997.

Monroe, Judy. *The Facts about Censorship.* New York: Crestwood House, 1990.

Munro, Kathryn. "Filtering Utilities." *PC Magazine,* April 8, 1997.

New York Public Library. *Censorship: 500 Years of Conflict.* New York: Oxford University Press, 1984.

Noble, William. *Bookbanning in America: Who Bans Books?—And Why?* Middlebury, Vt.: Paul S. Eriksson, 1990.

Orme, William A. "Reporters in Peril." *World Press Review,* April 1997.

Orr, Lisa, ed. *Censorship.* San Diego: Greenhaven Press, Inc., 1990.

Osanka, Franklin Mark, and Sara Lee Johann. *Sourcebook on Pornography.* Lexington, Mass.: Lexington Books, 1989.

Pascoe, Elaine. *Freedom of Expression: The Right to Speak Out in America, Issue and Debate.* Brookfield, Conn.: The Millbrook Press, 1992.

People for the American Way. "Artsave Helps Fourth-Grade Student." *PFAW News,* Fall 1996.

Reid, Calvin, and Bridget Kinsella. "In Banned Books Week, Censorship Still Thrives." *Publishers Weekly,* September 23, 1996.

Rheingold, Howard. *The Virtual Community: Homesteading on the Electronic Frontier.* Reading, Mass.: Addison-Wesley Publishing Company, 1993.

Rosen, Nancy. "Indecent Proposal." *Video Magazine,* February-March 1997.

Saltzman, Joe. "High School Journalism: Downsized into Oblivion." *USA Today,* January 1997.

Steele, Philip. *Censorship, Past and Present.* New York: New Discovery Books, 1992.

"Student's Fight for Decency Denounced as Censorship." *Education Reporter,* February 1994.

Taylor, C. L. *Censorship.* New York: Franklin Watts, 1986.

"Transcripts of Supreme Court, Janet Reno, *Attorney General of the United States et al vs. American Civil Liberties Union,* No. 96-511, March 19, 1997," <http://www.aclu.org/issues/cyber/trial/sctran.html> (1997).

Walsh, Frank. *Sin and Censorship: The Catholic Church and the Motion Picture Industry.* New Haven, Conn.: Yale University Press, 1996.

West, Mark I. *Trust Your Children: Voices against Censorship in Children's Literature.* New York: Neal-Schuman Publishers, 1988.

White, Cheryl, and Heather Moors Johnson. "My Son Built a Bomb," *Ladies Home Journal,* March 1997.

Wirth, Eileen. "The State of Censorship." *American Libraries,* September 1996.

Wolper, Allan. "Administrators as Censors: Student Press Law Center Director Mark Goodman Warns Student Journalists to Monitor Their Internet Copy." *Editor & Publisher,* 1996.

Zeinert, Karen. *Free Speech: From Newspapers to Music Lyrics.* Springfield, N.J.: Enslow Publishers, 1995.

Index

About the Author

Nancy Day is an accomplished writer who specializes in nonfiction for young audiences. She has published several books, is a member of the Society of Children's Book Writers and Illustrators, and received the society's Merit Award for Nonfiction in 1995. Her work has appeared in publications for children and adults, including *Cobblestone, Calliope, Dolphin Log, Highlights for Children, Hopscotch,* and *Odyssey,* and in various educational materials. Day has a B.A. from the University of Maryland and an Executive M.B.A. from Loyola College, Baltimore.

Photo Acknowledgments

John Marshall, Impact Visuals 6; Library of Congress 9, 21 (upper right); Archive Photos 10, 65; Richard B. Levine 13, 53, 56, 74 (lower right), 78, 79; Frances M. Roberts 16 (upper left); Catherine Smith/Impact Visuals 16 (lower left); Imperial War Museum/Archive Photos 18; Corbis-Bettman 21 (lower left); The New York Public Library, General Research Division 22; Corbis/Bettman-UPI 25; Rick Reinhard, Impact Visuals 28; Hollywood Book and Poster 30, 50, 98 (both); © 1958 by Garth Williams, used by permisson of HarperCollins Publishers 31; AP/Wide World Photos 32, 35, 38 (both), 61, 86; American Booksellers Foundation for Freedom of Expression 37; Motion Picture Association of America 42; © Daniel Sheehan 45; The Museum of Modern Art/Film Stills Archive 46, 51; Kevin J. Larkin/Corbis Bettmann 54; Kerstin Coyle/IPS 60; Visuals Unlimited/Jeff Greenberg 68; Net Nanny Software International, Inc. 74 (upper left); Baldwin H. Ward/Corbis-Bettman 80; © New Wave Photography/Nancy Erickson 83; Reuters/Archive Photos 88; *Ken Moody and Robert Sherman,* 1984 © The Estate of Robert Mapplethorpe. Used by permission 90; © 1991 Kirk Condyles/Impact Visuals 92; Charles D. Hogan/New York Times Pictures 94; UPI/Corbis-Bettman 97; Nancy Day Sakaduski 112.